Pastoral Care and Western Medicine

Christopher W. Bogosh

PRESS

Pastoral Care and Western Medicine
by Christopher W. Bogosh

Printed in the United States of America

ISBN 978-1-60791-803-5

www.xulonpress.com

What is thy only comfort in life and death?

That I with body and soul, both in life and death, am not my own, but belong unto my faithful Savior Jesus Christ; who, with His precious blood, hath fully satisfied for all my sins, and delivered me from all the power of the devil; and so preserves me that without the will of my heavenly Father, not a hair can fall from my head; yea, that all things must be subservient to my salvation, and therefore, by His Holy Spirit, He also assures me of eternal life, and makes me sincerely willing and ready, henceforth, to live unto Him.

Heidelberg Catechism

Table of Contents

Introduction ix

1. Western Medicine is NOT Neutral! 13

2. Becoming a Part of the Healthcare Team 37

3. Body, Soul, Medications, and Biblical Counseling 41

4. Making Decisions Regarding Medical Care 63

5. Pastoral Care and Counseling at End of Life 81

Appendices 95

A. Pastor's Medical Care Handbook 97

B. Medicine for the Body and Soul: "Songs in
   the Night" 109

C. Thomas Halyburton: A Story of Reality and Hope 119

D. The Christian and Advance Directives 131

E. Forever in His Sight: What to Expect as
   a Person Approaches Death 141

F. Going into God's Presence...147

G. Life's Final Trial: Devotions for Faith,
   Hope, and Assurance...155

Introduction

One of the things I have noticed over my twenty-year engagement to the healthcare system is the lack of conservative evangelical seminarians who are involved in the medical community. I have met many pastoral interns from liberal seminaries, but I have never met one from a conservative seminary. Perhaps this is due to the places I have lived, but I believe this problem may be more pervasive. Many conservative evangelical seminaries provide excellent training in the fundamentals of biblical theology, systematic theology, historical theology, and components of practical theology, but very few have courses dedicated to applied pastoral care in a medical setting. Due to this lack of exposure, many conservative evangelical pastors do not posses the fundamental skills and experience necessary to understand the complex world of Western medicine and the ability to work within its context.

To the shame of the conservative evangelical community, the liberal community has excelled in this area. Liberal seminaries have mandatory courses that assist their pastors in engaging the world of medicine. Unfortunately, the liberal zeal lacks a biblical worldview. The evangelical community must realize that Christian warfare needs to be fought on all fronts, and Western medicine is one front that cannot be given over to the enemy. There are godless, powerful, deceitful, destructive, and hopeless philosophies at work in the world of medicine, and the pastor must know how to counteract these principalities if he is to protect and guide the members of his congregation.

Often the church attacks the medical community for pushing the Christian community out of medical affairs, but I believe the blame rests equally on both sets of shoulders. In our culture of "departmental specialists," the church has been willing to let medical professionals do their work while the church specialists do theirs. In the past this was not always the case, however, as the names of so many reputable hospitals testify (i.e., New England Baptist, New York Presbyterian Hospital, etc.). The church has to recognize that medicine is not practiced in a vacuum. For this reason alone, the pastor must know how to respond to, and interact with, the medical community biblically, and that is why specific education for the pastor in this area is crucial.

When the pastor is uneducated and unengaged with the world of medicine, he is unable to communicate with medical professionals on the level he needs to for the sake of the members of his congregation. As a result, the pastor becomes intimidated and withdraws. He makes ignorant assumptions about medical care and becomes retaliatory and overly critical toward the medical community, or he will make personal experiences, and not biblical truth, normative. The member in the pew senses the pastor's ignorance in this area and as a result does not seek the pastor for care and counsel on medical matters. Instead, the ill or diseased member turns to the medical community for "real" help first and to the pastor for helpful prayer second. The ill-equipped pastor does not possess the ability to connect with the medical community intelligently, nor does he have the biblical guidance necessary for some of the most important questions a member in his congregation may ever have.

In the following pages, I will present a course of study for *Pastoral Care and Western Medicine.* The topics of our study are as follows:

- Western Medicine is NOT Neutral!
- Becoming a Part of the Healthcare Team.
- Body, Soul, Medications, and Biblical Counseling.
- Making Decisions Concerning Medical Care.
- Pastoral Care and Counseling at End of Life.

Ideally, this study would be greatly enhanced by exposure to a variety of healthcare settings and participation on various medical ethics committees.[1]

One

Western Medicine is NOT Neutral!

The Philosophy of Western Medicine

A round the world, ill health, infections, and death are viewed from a variety of perspectives that are influenced by culture, religion, philosophy, and science. In the West, for the most part, these afflictions are seen in a naturalistic and evolutionary context by Western medicine.

Naturalism can be dated back to the pre-Socratic philosophers, particularly to a man called Thales of Miletus (ca. 624-546 BC). Thales is considered the father of naturalistic science. His goal was to find physical explanations for events in the world without reference to the supernatural. As a scientific discipline, however, naturalism can be traced back directly to the ideas of some scholastic thinkers in the fourteenth century. Jean Buridan (ca. 1295-1358) and Nicole Oresme (ca. 1320-1382) were two clergymen who sought to counteract the rampant superstitions of their day through the use of naturalistic explanations. In the sixteenth and seventeenth centuries, naturalism would gain incredible momentum under such well-known figures as Francis

Bacon (1561-1626), Galileo Galilei (1564-1642), René Descartes (1596-1650), Baruch Spinoza (1632-1677), and Isaac Newton (1643-1727). During this time, naturalism was popularized and went on to inspire such notables as Charles Darwin (1809-1882) and Thomas Huxley (1825-1895).

Baruch Spinoza is one of the most influential figures in the philosophy of Western medicine. Spinoza was unique in his day, because he was the first modern philosopher to reject theology in the name of science. Most of the four-teenth-, sixteenth-, and seventeenth-century figures saw two books of life: nature and the Bible. Spinoza rejected this distinction outright and believed that through the use of scientific inquiry, everything that needed to be explained could be explained by appeal to the physical universe. Thus, he saw the universe as a closed system with no transcendent being and teleological end. The consequence of his theory was a view of life that was meaningless, mechanistic, and determined by nature. He also believed that all of nature was composed of one single substance, which he called "nature" or "god." This theory resulted in the doctrines of materialism, monism, and pantheism. Spinoza also suggested that human well-being is found in the ability of human beings to overcome the environment they live in—a doctrine observed later in Darwin's struggle for survival in which, according to Darwin, "the fittest win out at the expense of their rivals." The effect Spinoza has had on the philosophy of Western medicine cannot be overstated.

It is impossible to have a philosophical system totally confined to the physical universe, which is what naturalism tries to do. Whenever an unknown is postulated—such as, Why do I get sick? Who am I? Why am I here? What will happen after I die?—a metaphysical idea must be asserted. Because the naturalistic doctrines mentioned earlier do not give satisfactory answers for these ultimate questions, the department of psychology sought a remedy to this need by developing a synergistic system that embraces naturalism, spiritualism, and polytheism.

The giants of this newfound spirituality are Sigmund Freud (1856-1939), Carl Jung (1875-1961), and Abraham Maslow (1908-1970). Paul Vitz, in his book *Psychology as Religion*, draws a link between these men and the spiritualism that is found in contemporary New Age thinking. He writes, "These psychologists created a whole climate of opinion that made the unconscious, interior world seem more real than the conscious mind, with awareness of external reality."[1] In this system of belief, one must tap into his inner being in order to find the answers to life, death, and the hereafter.

In his book *Motivation and Personality*, first published in 1954 and revised in 1970, Abraham Maslow presented a hierarchy of human needs for personality development. At the pinnacle of this pyramid of development is what he calls a self-actualized state—that is the state in which one has total conscious awareness of the unconscious self, and vice versa. "This peak experience is a transcendent experience of oneness and wholeness and unity with the cosmos," writes Vitz, "and Maslow explicitly states that this experience is a natural—not a supernatural—phenomenon."[2] Thus, the synergism between the material and "immaterial" was achieved.

As defined by Vitz, the major beliefs found in the New Age creed are as follows:
- All is one: the doctrine of monism.
- All is god: the doctrine of pantheism.
- Human beings can become self-actualized.
- Lack of knowledge prevents us from realizing our inner divinity and, therefore, our divine destiny.
- All religions are one: polytheism.
- A hearty optimism about the present state of the world and humankind.

New Age assumes that humanity, because of its newfound God-consciousness, is on an evolutionary trajectory. Humanity is at the verge of a great transformation that will usher in a new era of peace, unity, and bliss.[3]

Christians Affirm the Following, Contrary to Western Medicine:
- General (natural) and special (supernatural) revelation, and through special revelation a philosophy about nature is developed.
- The universe is not a closed system; the LORD is sovereign over all, and the end will come when Jesus Christ returns.
- Life is purposeful and is determined by the mysterious providence of God.
- Nonliving objects are composed of material substance, but living creatures are composed of both material and immaterial substances.
- God is transcendent over and immanent in his creation.
- Human well-being is found in one's spiritual state with God, not in his physical state in the environment in which he lives.

Christians Reject the Following:
- The assumption that our universe consists of one substance (monism).
- The assumption that all is god and god is everything.
- The belief that human beings can become self-actualized.
- The belief that we possess inner divinity and are therefore intrinsically good.

- The assumption that all religions are basically the same and it does not matter what you believe (deism).
- The assumption that mankind has evolved and is still evolving, and through the exercise of our inbred god-consciousness, we will bring about tranquility, harmony, and happiness.

Although the department of psychology has attempted to put a positive spin on the underlying philosophy of Western medicine, its results are just as dismal. Consider three of the consequences of the assumptions listed above.

First, if life is only a series of meaningless cause-and-effect events with no teleological end, then what are we to make of our human existence? In such a system, it is impossible to find any meaning or goal to life, even if it is to be found in one's individualistic inner experience as humanistic psychology asserts!

Second, if all of nature (including human beings and God) is composed of one and the same substance, then what about those seemingly immaterial and abstract functions we have—functions such as conscious existence and unconscious experience: dreams, thoughts, desires, our love and affinity for one person over another, the concept of beauty, etc.? Are we to believe that these abstract entities are composed of a certain arrangement of electrons governed by the laws of physics, that these experiences are mere epiphenomena? In such a system, life is not only meaningless; it is senseless.

Third, what if a human being cannot survive in the environment in which he lives? Should we relegate him to the biological waste dump? What about infants, the elderly, those in a coma, the mentally retarded, the paralyzed, etc., all of whom are dependent upon the environment around them for survival? This is a cruel doctrine, but in our culture today it is a reality that is cloaked in such words as pro-choice, persistent vegetative state (PVS), and euthanasia.

When the assumptions of naturalism and humanistic psychology are considered authoritative and, therefore, normative for medical science, a system of belief emerges that is paradoxical, determined, impersonal, mechanistic, meaningless, and hopeless. In such a system, human life is nothing more than a differentiated piece of primordial substance that did not mutate into a virus or bacterium. It is logically impossible to possess true concepts of health, wellness, and life in this system of belief. The only hope medical science can give is the hope of pushing off the inevitable—illness, disease, suffering, pain, and death—for hours, days, months, years, or decades. But one day illness, disease, and death will strike, and the devotee of such a system will experience firsthand the hopelessness that this system truly espouses.

Western medicine will *never* succeed in truly treating or explaining the etiology of illness, disease, or death. The best it can do is to treat symptoms, extend life for a period of time, and provide placating and illusory answers that are restricted to the physical universe, based upon individualistic experience. How does medical science answer when a patient asks, "Why am I sick?" "Why did I contract this disease?" "Why am I going to die?" Based upon naturalism, evolution, and humanistic psychology, the answer has to be, "This is simply the way life is. We may be able to help you for a period of time, but one day all our help will end. At this time, you will die and be ushered off into—well that's up to you." After all the treatment options have been exhausted, a variation of this answer is the only one Western medicine has to offer, and it is an answer that is radically anti-Christian. So what is the Christian answer?

Western Medicine Informed Biblically
Creation in the Image of God

The Bible begins by asserting that God created everything, including humans, by a deliberate act (Gen. 1:1). The world and all of mankind was free from infectious diseases, pathologic conditions, genetic abnormalities, and death at this time—all was wellness, health, and life.[4] At the summit of God's creative activity, human beings were made (Gen. 1:26-27). This act was so significant and praiseworthy that it was immortalized by the first verse of poetic praise occurring in the Bible: "So God created man in his own image, in the image of God he created him; male and female he created them" (Gen. 1:27). Indeed, praise was in order because everything that God had made was blissfully perfect, and sickness, disease, suffering, pain, misery, and death were nonexistent. Everything was good—indeed it was "very good" (Gen. 1:31)!

The primary passages dealing with the creation and propagation of mankind are found in Genesis 2:7, 22, and 4:1: "The LORD God formed the man from the dust of the ground and breathed into his nostrils the breath of life, and the man became a living being"; "The LORD God made a woman from the rib he had taken out of the man, and he brought her to the man"; and "Adam lay with his wife Eve, and she became pregnant and gave birth to Cain." In 2:7 we are told that God "formed" the first man, deliberately, from part of the material universe, the "dust of the ground," and then he exhaled into the man an immaterial substance called "the breath [*ruach* = spirit] of life." After this creative action, man became a "living being [*nephesh* = soul]." In 2:22 we read that the first woman was made from a part of the material substance of man, and she was brought to the man as a living being (see diagram 2:1). As for the ages of the first man and woman, the Bible is silent, but they were old enough to reproduce, so it appears that they were young adults. In 4:1 we read that "Adam lay with his wife Eve and she became pregnant and gave birth to Cain." The first infant is brought into the world through the act of coitus between the man and woman, and he is composed of the material substance from both parents and an immaterial soul given by God (see diagram 2:2).[5]

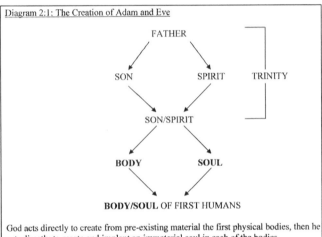

Diagram 2:1: The Creation of Adam and Eve

FATHER

SON   SPIRIT   TRINITY

SON/SPIRIT

BODY   SOUL

BODY/SOUL OF FIRST HUMANS

God acts directly to create from pre-existing material the first physical bodies, then he acts directly to create and implant an immaterial soul in each of the bodies.

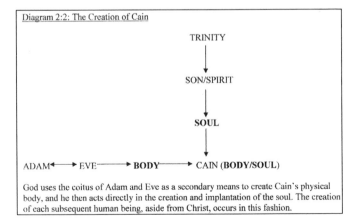

Diagram 2:2: The Creation of Cain

TRINITY

SON/SPIRIT

SOUL

ADAM◄──► EVE ──────► BODY ──────► CAIN (BODY/SOUL)

God uses the coitus of Adam and Eve as a secondary means to create Cain's physical body, and he then acts directly in the creation and implantation of the soul. The creation of each subsequent human being, aside from Christ, occurs in this fashion.

The Hebrew terms used to describe the immaterial substance in mankind are *nephesh*, usually translated "soul," and *ruah*, frequently translated "spirit" (cf. Gen. 2:7). The first term, "soul," occurs 754 times in the Old Testament, and it has three basic meanings: (1) the principle of life, (2) the part of man that departs at death, and (3) several figurative uses. The second term, "spirit," occurs 361 times in the Old Testament, and the semantic range is much broader: (1) God's Spirit, (2) angels, (3) the principle of life in humans and animals, (4) disembodied spirits, (5) breath, (6) wind, (7) disposition or attitude, (8) the seat of emotions, and (9) the seat of the mind and will in humans. A definite overlap exists between the two terms, and in the context of Genesis 2:7, the terms are virtually synonymous. The words refer to the immaterial principle of life that God has placed, not only in human beings, but also in all living creatures.

A significant term in the Old Testament that differentiates human beings from other creatures is *leb* or *lebab*, "heart." This term occurs 814 times in the Hebrew Bible with the following meanings: (1) the fleshy organ, (2) the seat of vital life force, (3) one's inner being, (4) inclination and disposition, (5) determination and courage, (6) will and intention, (7) attention, consideration and reason, (8) mind, (9) conscience, and (10) various other metaphorical meanings. John Cooper, in his book *Body, Soul & Life Everlasting*, describes the significance of this term when he writes:

> The heart in Hebrew thought is not significant primarily for its role in organic existence, but as the hidden control-center of the whole human being. The entire range of conscious and perhaps even unconscious activities of the person is located in and emanates from the heart. It experiences emotions and moods, it has personality and character traits, it is the locus of thought and deliberation, choice and action,

and it is above all the source of love or hate of God and neighbor.[6]

The "soul," "spirit," and "heart" are intricately inter-woven in the human constitution; they should not be dissected or isolated but seen as a unitary whole.

The crucial dissimilarity between human beings and other creatures is that humans are created in the image of God, and animals are not.

Then God said, "Let us make man in our image, in our likeness, and let them rule over the fish of the sea and the birds of the air, over the livestock, over all the earth, and over all the creatures that move along the ground." So God created man in his own image, in the image of God he created him; male and female he created them. (Gen. 1:26-27)

"God was the original of which man was made a copy," writes Louis Berkhof.[7] This means that *all* human beings not only *bear* the image of God but also represent God in their bodily existence. It is the immaterial part of man, the "soul," "spirit," or "heart," that *gives rise to* the image of God in man. Charles Hodge writes:

God is a Spirit, the human soul is a spirit. The essential attributes of a spirit are reason, conscience, and will. A spirit is rational, moral, and therefore also, a free agent. In making man after his own image, therefore, God endowed him with those attributes which belong to his own nature as a spirit. Man is thereby distinguished from all other inhabitants of this world, and raised immeasurably above them. He belongs to the same order of being as God Himself, and is therefore capable of communion with his Maker.[8]

It is important to note that the Bible says that the *entire* man, both the immaterial and material parts, was created in the image of God. The material body is the "instrument for the expression of the soul," writes Berkhof again, and the physical body was designed "to become a spiritual body; that is, a body which is completely spirit-controlled, a perfect instrument of the soul."[9]

In order to understand more fully the image of God in mankind, we need to study the relationship between the image of God and the Son of God. Meredith Kline comments: "Image of God and son of God" are "twin concepts."[10] This assertion is supported by citing the birth record of Seth in Genesis 5:1-3 and the later genealogical record in Luke's Gospel of the divine Son, Jesus. In Luke 3:38 we read that Jesus, the incarnate Son of God, is the "son of Seth, the son of Adam, the son of God." Kline writes:

> The eternal, firstborn Son furnished a pattern for man as a royal glory-image of the Father. It was in his creative action as the Son, present in the Glory-Spirit, making man in his own son-image that the Logos revealed himself as the One in whom was the life that is the light of men (John 1:4). Not first as incarnated Word breathing on men the Spirit and re-creating them in his heavenly image, but at the very beginning he was a quickening Spirit, creating man after his image and glory.[11]

What Kline is alluding to is that Jesus, the divine Son and second Adam, provides the purposed pattern for the image of God in mankind, not only in his incarnate state but also in his preincarnate state. It is the creative action of Jesus as the eternal "Word," along with the Spirit at the beginning, who implanted and stamped, as it were, the image of God on and in mankind, and this image is revealed centuries later in his incarnation (see diagrams 2:1 and 2:2). Kline simply echoes the words of John.

> In the beginning was the Word, and the Word was with God, and the Word was God. He was with God in the beginning. Through him all things were made; without him nothing was made that has been made. In him was life, and that life was the light of men. ... [He is the] true light that gives light to every man ... coming into the world ... The Word became flesh and made his dwelling among us. We have seen his glory, the glory of the One and only, who came from the Father.[12]

The eternal Son of God and the Spirit of God are the image of God the Father, as well as the dual agents who create and give rise to the life and the image of God in mankind.

This leads us to ask the question: what exactly is the image of God in mankind? The answer to this question has four aspects. First, man has been endowed with life. God is a living God, and he is the author of life. Second, mankind has been granted the capacity to rule and exercise justice over the creation. In Genesis 1:26a, we are invited into the deliberations of the heavenly throne room, where we hear the decision to make man in the image of God. The referents are not described, but what is significant is the action of the council. This suggests, as Kline notes, that "to bear the image of God is to participate in the judicial function of the divine Glory" (cf. Gen. 3:22). Also, in this same verse, mankind is granted universal rule over the creation under God. Third, human beings possess reason, conscience, and will. This is the "light" of the Word and Spirit that is given to mankind. Fourth, mankind possesses immortality, "not merely in the sense that [mankind] was endowed with an endless existence, but also in the sense that [mankind] did not carry within [it] the seeds of physical death."[13] In the *imago Dei*, we observe that the eternal Son and Spirit reveal and communicate life, the attributes of justice, rule, reason, conscience, will, and immortality to the souls of mankind in order for mankind to give expression to God's glorious image in his or her bodily existence (see diagram 2:3).

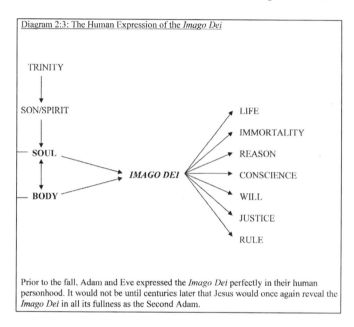

Diagram 2:3: The Human Expression of the *Imago Dei*

Prior to the fall, Adam and Eve expressed the *Imago Dei* perfectly in their human personhood. It would not be until centuries later that Jesus would once again reveal the *Imago Dei* in all its fullness as the Second Adam.

It is important to recognize the unity of the body and soul in human personhood—both were created as an integrated and inseparable unit. It was only after death entered into the world, as we will study later, that a dichotomy, or separation, occurred between the body and soul. Therefore, the material body and immaterial soul function together as a harmonious entity. As J. P. Moreland and S. B. Rae comment, *"The body is in the soul and the soul is in the body."*

The soul is a substantial, unified reality that informs its body. At a minimum, in some ways the soul is to the body like God is to space—it is fully "present" at each point. The soul occupies the body, but it is not spatially located within it. Further, the soul stands under, unifies, informs and makes human the body.[14]

The soul does not merely occupy the body, as a clam does a shell, but it transcends it. So if you lose a part of your body, you will not lose part of your soul. The soul, although not locally present in the body, is still *with* the body in order to inform and animate it. Moreland and Rae comment:

On this view, function determines form and not vice versa. The various teleological functions latent within the soul are what guide the development of and ground the spatially extended structure of inseparable parts (the body). Thus the substantial soul is a whole that is ontologically prior to the body and its various inseparable parts. The various physical and chemical parts and processes (including DNA) are tools—instrumental causes employed by higher-order biological activities in order to sustain the various functions grounded in the soul. Thus the soul is the first efficient cause of the body's development as well as the final cause of its functions and structure internally related to the soul's essence. The functional demands of the soul's essence determine the character of the tools, but they, in turn, constrain and direct the various chemical and physical processes that take place in the body.[15]

Put simply, the soul animates the body, and the body expresses the action of the soul, even at the microscopic level; although the soul is always prior to the body and transcends the body, the two exist as a unitary whole.

Cooper, following the late philosopher and theologian Herman Dooyeweerd (1894-1977), describes the human body as an intricate set of increasingly comprehensive structures and functions, dependent upon the emanating life force of a God-created soul. At the most basic level, there are atomic particles, chemicals, proteins, DNA, etc. These are the simplest structures in the human body that retain functionality. They, in turn, form the next level of structure with functionality, namely, the bodily organism, or the entire physical body itself, the brain, heart, lungs, liver, etc. The bodily organism also preserves its own makeup and functions, and it makes possible the next level of structure, which is the neuropsychological level. This level includes such material or neurological functions as neurotransmission and electrical conduction and such immaterial or psychological functions as consciousness, rationality, intellectual power, emotions, feelings, desires, etc. The fourth and final level is called the act-structure. At this level there exists an "interrelated set of intentional operations" of the soul, which are internal, such as deliberating, choosing, imagining, etc., and external such as activity in work, worship, socializing, creating art, serving others, etc.[16] At each level of bodily structure, there are certain functions that are dependent upon prior structures and functions, all of which are ultimately dependent on the soul. It is this unity of body and soul, at each structural and functional level, that makes human beings human (see diagram 2:4).

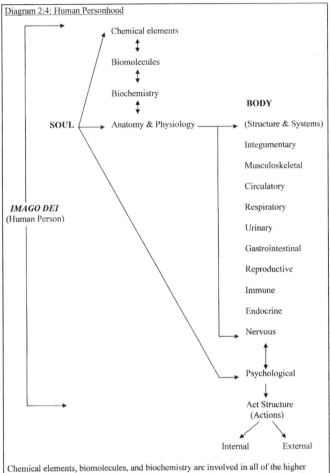

Diagram 2:4: Human Personhood

Chemical elements, biomolecules, and biochemistry are involved in all of the higher anatomical and physiological structures and functions of the body. The soul is the first and final cause of all bodily structures, systems, and actions. At the neuropsychological level material (neurological; bodily) functions become immaterial (psychological; soulish) processes, and vice versa.

We can only exclaim with the psalmist, "I praise you because I am fearfully and wonderfully made; your works are wonderful, I know that full well" (Ps. 139:14). This is biblical anthropology at its best! But now we leave the heights of our created glory to plumb the depths of human depravity as we investigate the etiology of illness, disease, and death.

The Etiology of Illness, Disease, and Death

The etiology of illness, disease, and death in Western medicine is built on an evolutionary paradigm. Basically, this view holds that life started on the earth in molecular form and evolved into cells that contain genetic material called DNA. In the course of cell division, the DNA underwent random aberrations known as mutations. Some of these genetic abnormalities resulted in illness and death for the cells. Other mutations gave rise to cells that became deadly agents like viruses and bacteria. Still other mutations caused the evolution of complex organisms, resulting eventually in a plethora of different species, including *Homo sapiens*, or human beings. In a nutshell, illness, disease, and death are the result of blind natural forces that are woven into the very fabric of our existence.

According to the majority opinion in Western medicine, this is the way life is, and it was never any other way. Ailments, infections, the eventual extinction of our physical bodies, and all the pain and suffering that go along with them are part and parcel of who we are. We cannot escape these conditions. Ironically, it is the mission and final goal of medical science to hunt down and eradicate these enemies. There is a paradox at this point that Western medicine cannot explain. If these enemies are woven into the very fabric of our existence, how can they be eradicated?

The Christian has to reject the premise for these assumptions, because they are radically antibiblical. The answer the Bible gives for the etiology of illness, disease, and death resides in the metaphysical realm, which is why the appeal to special revelation is crucial. The Scriptures speak with clarity on the subject: "God made mankind upright, but men have gone in search of many schemes" and the result, among other things, was illness, disease, and death (Eccles. 7:29).

Thomas Boston (1676-1732), in his book *Human Nature in Its Fourfold State*, explains:

> Man was made right (agreeable to the nature of God, whose work was perfect), without any imperfection, corruption, or principle of corruption, in his body or soul. He was made "upright" that is, straight with the will and law of God, without any irregularity in his soul ... [man was] directly pointed towards God, as his chief end . . . [and was] altogether righteous, pure, and holy. God made him thus: He did not first make him, and then make him righteous, but in the very making of him, He made him righteous. Original righteousness was created with him; so that in the same moment he was a man, he was a righteous man, morally good; with the same breath that God breathed into him a living soul, He breathed into him a righteous soul.[17]

The problem at the heart of illness, disease, and death is not physical or natural—the problem is moral. God created mankind in such a way that every part of his body and soul was impeccably righteous to the core, but mankind devised another plan, and as a result, he rebelled against his Creator and suffered the consequences.

The righteousness of man is not independent from God, but is dependent upon him. "God made man habitually righteous," writes Boston, but now man must exercise his free will and make himself and all his descendents, "actually righteous."[18] In order to accomplish this, God gave Adam a test of loyalty and devotion. In Genesis 2:16-17 we read, "You are free to eat from any tree in the garden; but you must not eat from the tree of the knowledge of good and evil, for when you eat of it you will surely die." In this test, which is referred to as the Covenant of Life, God requires dedicated obedience to him. If Adam passed the test, he and all his descendents would be blessed and live on in eternal bliss forever; if not, they would be cursed and die. The Covenant of Life was a test of Adam's love, faithfulness, and fidelity to God, as well as his contentment with God's righteous and moral standards.

The "tree of the knowledge of good and evil" was a symbol of all moral knowledge and, therefore also of sovereign judicial power and dominion. It was knowledge that God alone had the right to possess and that the creature was to be dependent upon the Creator to receive. Bruce Waltke, in his commentary on *Genesis*, writes:

> Only God in heaven, who transcends time and space, has the prerogative to know truly what is good and bad for life. Thus, the tree represents knowledge and power appropriate only to God (Gen. 3:5, 22). Human beings, by contrast, must depend upon a revelation from the only one who truly knows good and evil (Prov. 30:1–6).[19]

The other tree in the garden, "the tree of life," symbolized mankind's potential for life in its highest blessing. Again, Waltke comments, "In Proverbs 'tree of life' is used to refer to anything that heals, enhances, and celebrates life: righteousness (11:30), longing fulfilled (13:12), and a tongue that brings healing (15:4)."[20] Adam and Eve were free to "eat from any tree in the garden" and presumably even from the "tree of life," but instead they chose the "tree of the knowledge of good and evil." The result was "death." All human beings became dead to God, the author of life, and physical illness, disease, and physical death entered the world.

The violation of the Covenant of Life resulted in the curse of God on the entire creation, and all of mankind was plunged into a state of sin, misery, and death. The bodies and souls of human beings were polluted to the core. At every level of the human person—the immaterial soul, and the physical structures and functional states of the body—every part was corrupted. As a result, men and women no longer think God's thoughts after him. Life is denigrated. Justice is manipulated. Rule is abused. Reason is twisted. Conscience is hardened. Will is perverted. Human beings are no longer free to follow the ways of God but are enslaved to their depraved bodies and souls and the cursed creation around them. They can choose only those things that feed their own selfish desires and ends. The *imago Dei* is totally distorted and nearly destroyed!

The harmonious union of body and soul also was affected. After the rebellion, harmful viruses, bacteria, cancers, genetic mutations, agents of trauma, old age, and a plethora of other deadly agents entered the world—these are the harbingers of death. Why do we get sick and die? It is because of SIN! One day physical death will visit every human being, and its fatal blow will rip the harmonious unity of body and soul *unnaturally* asunder; and the soul will be transported to an eternal existence to await the second coming of Christ, and the resurrected reunification of the body and soul for final judgment. This leads us to ask a seemingly simple question: When does the soul no longer animate the body; that is, when is a person physically dead?

Physical Death Understood Biblically

Due to technological, mechanical, and pharmaceutical advances in Western medicine, the answer to this question is no longer easy. Until the middle of the twentieth century, death was defined as the absence of cardiac and respiratory function—a definition that is thoroughly biblical.[21] In the

1960s, however, it became increasingly possible to reverse cardiac and respiratory arrest through the use of cardiopulmonary resuscitation, defibrillation, mechanical ventilation, medications, and other treatments. Now, cardiac arrest and respiratory failure do not define death but rather a state called "clinical death."

According to the medical community, clinical death is a medical condition that precedes death. At the time of clinical death, the following events occur in the body. First, the heart stops beating, and the lungs stop breathing. Then, in a matter of minutes, all the tissues and organs of the body will incur an injury called *ischemia*. Second, within seconds of cardiopulmonary cessation, the person will lose consciousness; and in twenty to forty seconds, measurable brain activity will cease. If circulation and respiratory function are not restarted, the brain will suffer serious damage. Due to technological advances, the medical community has the ability to reverse this state, but it may be at the expense of brain function and consciousness. As a response to the ability to resuscitate individuals and keep them mechanically alive, "brain death" has now emerged as the legal definition of death.

In 1981 a presidential commission issued a landmark report called *Defining Death: Medical, Legal, and Ethical Issues in the Determination of Death*. This report is the basis for the "Uniform Definition of Death Act," which is now law in almost all fifty states. Using brain-death criteria, the medical community can declare a person legally dead, even if the body is alive but does not have supposed "brain function." The Act reads:

An individual who has sustained either (1) irreversible cessation of circulatory and respiratory functions, or (2) irreversible cessation of all functions of the entire brain, including the brain stem, is dead. A determination of death must be made in accordance with accepted medical standards.[22]

There are two difficulties with this act. First, the language is ambiguous. What does "irreversible" mean? And who or what decides what is irreversible? Second, a "determination of death" is "made in accordance with accepted medical standards," which are decisions based upon mechanical instruments, a medical doctor's subjective assessment, naturalism, and functionality. Needless to say, the "Uniform Definition of Death Act" is seriously flawed.

Biblically, a person is dead when the heart, lungs, and brain have ceased to function. If there is no breathing, no heartbeat, and no neurological function, the person is dead; the soul no longer animates the body. This means that if a person is on artificial life support and has been diagnosed as being "brain dead," it will be necessary to wean the person off of life support to see if the person is truly dead. If the apparatus is removed, however, and the heart and lungs function, then the person is not dead, even if the condition of the "brain dead" person is said to be "irreversible." In such cases a moral and ethical precedent has been set, and the vulnerable person's life must be sustained by feeding and caring for him, even if it means the insertion of a feeding tube (cf. Matt. 25:34-35). This does not mean, however, that aggressive medical treatment such as cardiopulmonary resuscitation, intravenous infusions, or other treatment modalities should be sought in the future to prolong life.

Clearly, there are serious moral, ethical, and philosophical concerns for the Christian in relation to Western medicine. These underlying principles will govern the care of many healthcare professionals and inform the regulations, policies, and procedures established by many healthcare institutions. The pastor must be aware of these matters and have a clear and unadulterated biblical response to them.

The Bible provides a glorious philosophy of human personhood, and it also explains clearly why we get sick and die.
Western medicine is not neutral! In fact, it presents a radically anti-Christian philosophy of human personhood, life,
illness, disease, and death. How may the pastor address these
concerns and assist his congregation? He can become a part
of the healthcare team.

Two

Becoming a Part of the Healthcare Team

Note: This section of the course would be greatly enhanced if a series of medical rotations in a variety of healthcare settings were implemented. The purpose of the rotations is to be exposed to the world of Western medicine in order to facilitate comfort and interaction with healthcare professionals.

Joining the Team

The pastor plays an important role on the healthcare team, but more often than not, he never becomes a part of the team. This is due, in some part, to church members' lack of education concerning the role of a pastor. For this reason, it is important for the pastor to teach his sheep about his shepherding role. He not only teaches and preaches but also provides biblical counsel, ministers to the sick, and guides and directs biblically. A church member should not seek a medical doctor's counsel alone but should seek it together with that of his pastor.

Although the pastor may provide all of his counseling directly to a member without participating face-to-face with the healthcare team, there may be times that face-to-face involvement will be extremely helpful. In order for the pastor to assist the member in this area, it will be necessary for the member to identify the pastor as someone he wants involved in his medical care. This identification may be accomplished by a simple introduction of the pastor to the medical team by the member, or it may require a written statement. State and federal laws mandate that healthcare professionals protect the confidentiality of their patients. So, again, it will be necessary for the member to identify the pastor as a person he wants to participate in his medical care and decisions. If this happens, the same laws require healthcare professionals to respect the patient's rights and to include the pastor on the healthcare team.

Depending on each individual case, the team will consist of a variety of healthcare professionals and will occur in a variety of settings. It is important to acknowledge and respect the roles and expertise of each of the team members. Although the underlying philosophy of Western medicine is radically anti-Christian and many of the professionals will be as well, medical science still provides diagnostics and treatments, and the healthcare professionals are experts in their respective fields of study. It is important to listen carefully to what these people have to say and to work together with them, while at the same time biblically weighing what they say.

Pointers for Working with Healthcare Professionals:
- Be humble, intelligent, and helpful.
- Don't have a critical spirit but be a critical thinker.
- Listen carefully to what team members have to say.
- Don't try to be the doctor or another member of the healthcare team—be the pastor.
- Know your limitations and the roles of other healthcare team members.

The Pastor and the Hospice Team

The most important healthcare team the pastor may be a part of is the hospice team. State and federal regulations recognize the importance of spiritual care at the end of life, so they require that all hospice programs provide spiritual care to their patients. The pastor has an open door to fill this role, and he should initiate this role immediately in the interest of the dying member and his or her family. He should be present at the initial hospice admission visit and be identified as the person managing the spiritual care. This important step will accomplish three things. First, it will allow the pastor to help direct the philosophy of care given. This is of utmost importance, as we will see later. Second, it will place the pastor in a position to communicate to the hospice agency on behalf of the dying member and family. This step will eliminate a lot of stress for patient and family, and assure biblically oriented care. Third, it will allow the pastor to counsel the dying member and family, thereby limiting unbiblical influences.

The pastor will need to explain his role clearly to the hospice team members. The core team members will include a physician, nurse, aides, social worker, and chaplain. Most, if not all, of the communication will occur through the nurse, but the other team members may be present as well. The pastor should explain the following. First, the congregation he serves will assist the dying member and his or her family with their social needs (i.e., visitation, meals, breathers, etc.). Second, he will provide *all* the necessary counseling for them, as well as the bereavement follow-up. Third, he will work with the other hospice team members in place of the chaplain to assist in the spiritual care of the dying member and the family. Nine times out of ten, if the pastor presents his role in a humble nonconfrontational way, the hospice team will not get defensive, and the team will appreciate the pastor's and the congregation's involvement.

The pastor also has the responsibility of integrating the congregation into the hospice team. First, the pastor needs to notify the diaconal team (if the congregation has one). The diaconal team will be able to assess the mercy and hospitality needs of the dying member and his or her family. Needs may include, but are not limited to, providing meals, setting up a visitation schedule, providing funds, providing breaks for family members, etc. Second, the pastor needs to pray publicly for the dying member and the family in specific ways. Prayer should occur during corporate worship and weekly prayer meetings. Third, the dying person and the person's family should be discussed at each session and deacon meeting. These discussions must include, but are not limited to, such topics as (1) how the dying member and the family are doing spiritually and physically; (2) what kind of assistance the church is giving—specifically, at what level the congregation is involved, whether the assistance is disseminated wisely, and what further assistance is needed; (3) what the hospice team is doing and how the integration is working; and (4) what the plan ahead is for the time of death, funeral arrangements, and bereavement follow-up.

It is crucial for the pastor to integrate into a variety of healthcare teams and settings. Medical rotations can prepare the pastor for integration with the healthcare team, but it will be the members of his congregation who facilitate that integration. Therefore, educating members about the pastor's shepherding role will be very important. One of the most significant and rewarding healthcare teams a pastor will ever be a part of is the hospice team. This will be an excellent opportunity to minister like Christ, to draw the congregation together, and to be a powerful testimony to the hospice team members. The pastor also will learn a great deal about the relationship between the body and soul and how medications may be used in counseling the afflicted.

Three

Body, Soul, Medications, and Biblical Counseling

I n this next section, we will attempt to study the obscure relationship between the body and the soul and the necessary dependency they have on one another in this present state of existence. We noted earlier that man is a unitary being, and he was created as an integrated and inseparable unit. It was only after death entered the world that a dichotomy occurred between body and soul. It is crucial for the pastor to recognize this biblical fact and understand clearly that the material body and immaterial soul function together as a harmonious entity. This unified state is the natural state of man, and both the body and the soul must be considered when counseling.

Body Meets Soul: Delirium

In order to study the relationship between the body and the soul, we will look at a medical condition called delirium. *Delirium* is a broad diagnostic term that is used to describe an acute state of confusion that may be caused by an underlying physiological or psychological problem. It has been called "reversible madness" and "everyone's psychosis," and it is the most common mental disorder encountered in hospitalized patients. "By definition," writes Dr. Robert E. Enck, "delirium is a transient disorder of cognition and attention, one accompanied by disturbances of the sleep-wake cycle and psychomotor activity."[1] Delirium may affect perception and cause a person to experience visual and auditory illusions. It may result in disorganized thinking, which will be evident in incoherent speech. A person's memory may be impaired, usually in regard to time and orientation to place. A delirious person may have attention and awareness deficits, be lethargic, and have a disturbed sleep-wake cycle. Psychomotor activity may be impaired, resulting in hypo- or hyperactive muscular action, which may lead to slow respirations, flaccidity, agitation, twitching, and seizures. A delirious person *will* experience a broad range of emotions such as giddiness, depression, apathy, fear, and rage. We will come back to delirium later, but let's lay some groundwork first.

The Relationship of the Body to the Soul and the Soul to the Body

It is obvious that one's psychological state, which is a soulish state, is affected by one's physical state, and vice versa. If I am dehydrated, I will suffer from a headache and experience the psychological state of pain. But if I take two Tylenols, drink a couple glasses of water, and lie down for a period of time, my headache will vanish, and my psychological state of pain will cease. The entire process of removing this psychological state, aside from the initial act of recognizing the pain and deciding to treat it, is a bodily function. I say to myself, "Wow, what a headache!" Then I think to myself, "I must be dehydrated. I will take a couple of Tylenols, drink some water, and lie down for a while." Then I go to the medicine cabinet, take out the Tylenols, fill up a cup of water, put the Tylenols into my mouth, and swallow them with a glass of water. I proceed to my bed, drink another glass of water, and lie down. As I lie in bed, the Tylenol is digested, processed by my liver, and absorbed into my bloodstream. The medicated blood is pumped by my heart to the neurological system, and the drug exerts a blockade effect on a certain part of my brain. The water hydrates my body, and the rest provides recuperation. Thus, when I rise thirty minutes later, my headache is gone, and the psychological state of pain is eliminated. I am refreshed, pain free, and ready to go!

By way of review, we noted that the body and the soul are intimately united. The material body and immaterial soul function together as one harmonious entity. We do not know what the soul is composed of, only that it is an immaterial, spiritual substance from God. Neither do we know how the immaterial soul and the material body communicate with one another, but only that somehow they do. We also noted that the soul is the life force of the body and its control center. The entire range of conscious and unconscious activities—moods, emotions, rationality, personality, morality, thought, deliberation, action, choice, and love or hate for God and neighbor—are found, ultimately, in the soul. It is the soul that gives rise to the image of God in one's bodily experience, and both the body and the soul are necessary for communion with God in this present state of existence. We also noted that God made the body to be the perfect immortal instrument of the soul, but the entrance of evil into the world has affected all of this.

We saw that the action of the soul occurs prior to the action of the body. That is, all the functions of the body and its various structures lie dormant in the soul. The entire body is the instrument of the soul, from the smallest molecules to the largest anatomical systems. The soul is the first efficient and final cause of bodily function and structure. Every goal, action, and purpose of every single bodily function is caused by, and initiated by, the soul's action.

We also noted that the human body is composed of a complex set of progressively comprehensive, intertwined structures that retain functionality at each level of existence. The first is at the molecular level, which consists of atomic particles, chemicals, proteins, DNA, etc. The second level is the bodily organism, the entire body itself: brain, heart, lungs, liver, etc. The third level is the neuropsychological level, which includes such bodily or neurological functions as neurotransmission and electrical conduction and such soulish or psychological functions as consciousness, rationality, intellectual power, emotions, feelings, and desires. The fourth and final level is called the act-structure. This includes the external bodily expressions of the soul in work, socializing, worship, loving one's neighbor, justice, exercising dominion, etc. and internal bodily expressions of the soul such as deliberating, choosing, and obeying. All the functions at the act-structure level express the intentionality of the soul. In the non-Christian, the soul, and therefore the body, is *always* driven by sin; in the Christian, it is driven either by sin or righteousness.

Dangers in Misunderstanding the Body-and-Soul Relationship

The soul is prior to the body in the sense that it gives the body life, consciousness, and intentionality; and without the soul, the body is lifeless. But this does not mean that the body does not influence the soul, as we have already noted briefly. There are two extremes that must be avoided at this point. The first suggests that psychological experience emanates only from neurological function, and the second suggests that it is only psychological experience that causes neurological function. These are two one-way streets that need to be avoided. The body and soul influence one another in a mysterious way, but the soul is always prior to the body, because it is the fountain of life, conscious existence, and intentionality.

Another tendency we need to avoid is compartmentalizing the soul. The soul is one simple substance with different functions, and distinctions between the heart and the mind must be avoided. The Bible is not clear in this area,[2] and in light of the progress in the neurological and psychological sciences, we have to admit that the whole relationship is extremely obscure and complicated. The greatest danger with a heart-mind dichotomy is the potential to fall into a form of behavioral psychology, which has been the plight of many biblical counseling models.

Recognizing this mutual influence of body and soul is significant because it means that bodily changes can cause a person to sin. For example, let's say I am suffering from the same headache mentioned earlier. But instead of treating the headache, I grit my teeth and bear the pain. As a result I become irritable, and I have a fit of anger aimed at my wife, an obvious act of outward sin. Or perhaps I am irritable (a state of discontentment, which is sin) because of my headache, and it causes me to have angry thoughts toward my wife, but I do not express them outwardly. This is an act of sin as well (cf. Matt. 5:21-22). Both responses arise from my psychological state of pain and irritability, which is caused by my headache due to the bodily problem of dehydration. In fact, the only way to refrain from sin in such a state is to have no sinful actions or thoughts at all, a feat that Christ alone can accomplish and the Christian can only strive after in grace.

Now let's consider the state of delirium mentioned earlier and the range of psychological and neurological changes that this will cause. Delirium, like every other illness, disease, trauma, and neuropsychological problem, exists because of the fall; so in this sense, it is evil—it is the result of original sin and the curse. The state, itself, however, does not make a person sinful (a person is sinful already), but it can cause a sinful person, even a renewed sinful person, to think and act in sinful ways. Delirium has caused some of the most devout Christians to think and act in ways that they themselves thought were impossible.

Case Study: Jim

Jim is a fifty-year-old married missionary with six children; his mission field is China. He was raised in a Christian home, was part of a healthy church, and never knew a day that he did not know the Lord. He was called to the mission field as a teenager, so in preparation he obtained a B.A. and M.Div., and he learned the Chinese language. He also made several short-term mission trips to China, which fueled his burden to serve God in that country. It was during one of those mission trips that he met his beloved wife Shirley. At the age of twenty-six, Jim and Shirley were called as full-time missionaries to China. The Lord blessed the couple's missionary work, and several congregations were planted with indigenous pastors trained by Jim.

On occasion, Jim was noted to have increased forgetfulness, periods of confusion, and altered sleep patterns—the symptoms of delirium mentioned earlier. Then, one day, after eating some beef, Jim slept the whole next day. He was very lethargic and confused, so much so, that he soiled his bed. The day following, Jim had a yellowish color to his skin, and he was extremely agitated and itchy. He got up out of bed and was staggering around his bedroom, confused and disoriented. In his stupor he repeatedly shouted, "Curse God for this itch! Curse God for this itch!" Shirley went to Jim, confronted his behavior, and attempted to help him back to bed. But when she approached, he swung wildly at her and said with a piercing gaze, "Get away from me, Jezebel!" Traumatized, afraid, and shocked, Shirley stepped back into the doorway of the room and stood there speechless. Soon

Jim staggered, fell on the bed, and went back to sleep. The local doctor saw Jim and diagnosed him with cirrhosis of the liver with hepatic encephalopathy.

Jim developed this condition from the Hepatitis A virus due to the poor hygienic conditions of the rural village he lived in. The hepatic encephalopathy was caused by increased ammonia levels and toxins in his blood, which affected his neuropsychological function and caused him to enter into a delirious state. This kind of behavior was totally uncharacteristic for Jim, who was a devout Christian and loved his wife dearly. The doctor treated Jim with a medication called lactulose and suggested a low-protein diet. Over the next couple of days, Jim recovered and returned to his baseline. Shirley asked Jim if he remembered what had happened, and he said that he did not. When she told him, he was shocked, dismayed, and ashamed. Jim repented of his sin and sought God's forgiveness and Shirley's forgiveness immediately. On the modified diet and lactulose, Jim was able to control the amount of ammonia in his blood and prevent any future bouts of hepatic encephalopathy, delirium, and the evil thoughts and behaviors caused by the disease.

In Jim's case, we see something very important—it is necessary to address bodily problems in order to address problems of the soul. In Jim's delirious state, it was impossible for him to modify his behavior—he didn't even know what he was doing! Regardless, Jim was still guilty of sin. "If a person sins and does what is forbidden in any of the LORD's commands, even though he does not know it, he is guilty and will be held responsible" (Lev. 5:17). Jim required medication to alleviate his underlying problem. Then, after his bodily need was met, the problem of his soul was addressed. Yes, the body is the instrument of the soul, but it is also important to recognize that the soul also is affected by the body. The two were made to work together as a holistic unity. So when the body is affected, the soul will be affected as well.

Body and Soul: Neurology and Psychology

At the neuropsychological level, bodily entities become soulish entities, and soulish entities become bodily entities. My hand touches a hot flame. In a matter of milliseconds, a neurotransmission occurs along the complex pathways of my systemic nerves, to my spinal cord, and up to my brain. The painful event becomes an abstract concept. It is registered, processed, felt, experienced, and evaluated. The reverse is also true. I can recall a painful experience from my memory, and the abstract concept can affect my body. Neurotransmission begins in my brain, travels to the spinal cord, and is sent to the systemic nerves. How I respond to the pain occurs at the act-structure level, which consists of the innumerable interrelated intentional actions of the soul that are expressed internally and externally. But prior to this point, the body and soul must first interact, and this requires neuropsychological integration.

John Bunyan, in his book *Holy War*, portrays the body and soul as a castle. In order to enter the interior of the castle, the soul, one must go through the Ear Gate or the Eye Gate. In a very real sense, the body is the doorway to the soul. It is through our five sensory organs—eyes, ears, nose, mouth, and skin—that we come into contact with those things outside of us. These are the neurological gateways and avenues to our psychological, or soulish, experiences.

Everything outside of us will exert its influence on our souls in some way. If I look upon a person who is dying from cancer, the sight will affect my psychological state. If I am diagnosed with a terminal illness, the news I hear will cause a psychological response. If I smell a putrid odor, I may feel queasy and sick. If I am racked with pain, the narcotic I swallow will exert its influence, not only on my neurological state, but also on my psychological state. If I am on my deathbed, the touch I feel from a loved one will affect me as well. Everything we come into contact with will be received, processed, and responded to in some way. If this were not the case, we could never experience communion with one another or with God, who has chosen to reveal himself to us in the creation and in the words of Holy Scripture.

When we were born again, God called us by his Spirit. It is a call that is consonant with the words of Scripture. Perhaps, it was the Word heard or read many years ago that was stored away in our memory banks.[3] Perhaps, it was hearing the preached Word that very moment. Possibly, it was seeing the Word lived out by a godly person. Whatever the case may be, the Word and the Spirit worked together to convert us. At a certain time, our hopeless condition of sin and misery was revealed, and the result of this revelation was the psychological state of conviction. We cried out, either silently or audibly, "What must I do to be saved?" Then the meaning of the words in Acts 16:31 became crystal clear: "Believe in the Lord Jesus, and you will be saved." The Holy Spirit reoriented our souls, and we gained true knowledge of the Bible. We were persuaded, enabled, and made willing by the Holy Spirit to embrace the historical Jesus by faith, as he was revealed in the pages of Holy Scripture.

The Holy Spirit and the Word of God

In order for communication to occur between God and man, God must facilitate the needs and capacity of man. Ronald Wallace writes, "God, in revealing Himself to man, has to transform Himself by covering over that in Himself which man . . . cannot bear to see, and [his] . . . mind is too small to grasp."[4] Therefore, God in his grace conceals his incomprehensible and radiant being by hiding himself in earthly signs and symbols that can be received by our sensory organs. These signs and symbols indirectly represent what God is communicating to man. In this way, God is able to transmit himself to mankind, and communication is made possible.

When God reveals himself, he attaches a sign to audible words. For example, God appeared to Moses in the burning bush and spoke (Exod. 3:2, 4). The bush signifies the presence of God, and it is from the bush that he speaks. The same principle works in reverse. The audible voice of God is attached to visible signs. For example, when Jesus is rebuking Satan in the wilderness, he says, "It is written, 'Man shall not live by bread alone, but by every word that comes from the mouth of God'" (Matt. 4:4). Jesus affirms the written words of Scripture (written words are signs) and says that they come from the mouth of God. It follows that revelation from God will have an objective sign attached to it.

The medium of *all* revelation between God and man is the Word of God, the Second Person of the Trinity, who is revealed in Holy Scripture. The Word of God is the fountain of all the visions, utterances, oracles, dreams, and prophecies mentioned in Scripture; it is also the Word of God who gives definition to all of God's earthly signs under the old and new covenants. Under the old covenant, the Word was revealed in theophanic forms. In the new covenant, the Word of God was revealed in the person of Jesus Christ (John 1:1). The coming of the Word in human form marked the pinnacle of all revelatory activity. The Word is the ultimate sign and means of redemption for mankind in every age.

The Scriptures present this special communication between the Word of God and mankind in three distinct contexts. First, it is presented in the eternal and incarnate *logos,* or "Word," Jesus Christ in the flesh. In John 1:1 the Greek reads: *En arche en ho logos* ("In the beginning was the Word," *kai ho logos en pros ton theon,* "and the Word was with God," *kai theos en ho logos,* "and God was the Word." The *logos* is distinct from God and yet one with God, and it is precisely for this reason that the *logos* can be God's medium of communication. Second, the verbal message was given to the prophets and the apostles of the Old and New Testaments (1 Pet. 1:21). The *logos* was communicated throughout human history in several ways. God spoke to the prophets and apostles in visions, utterances, oracles, and dreams. Third, the message of God was written down on the pages of the Old and New Testaments (2 Pet. 1:19). After God completed his message, the previous forms of authoritative communication ceased, and in order to preserve and propagate the truth, the divine *logos* was committed to writing on the pages of Holy Scripture. In all cases, and in every age, the eternal *logos* is the origin and foundation for God's objective communication with mankind.

The Holy Spirit must accompany the written Word of God in order to make it effectual in the soul, and this is accomplished most commonly in the act of preaching. "Preaching," writes Herman Bavinck "is the authoritative proclamation of the gospel by the church in the service of the Word of God through Christ."[5] In the act of preaching, you do not *hear about* the Word of God, but you *hear* the Word of God. In his comment on Isaiah 55:11, John Calvin writes, "The word *goeth out of the mouth* of God in such a manner that it likewise 'goeth out of the mouth' of men."[6] In a sense, the preacher is the conduit used by God to communicate his Word. The preacher expounds the written Word under the inspiration of the Holy Spirit, and the Word of God is communicated to the ears of mankind, either condemning or bringing life (2 Cor. 2:16).

The Word of God also must accompany the sacraments of baptism and the Lord's Supper. In his *Institutes of the Christian Religion,* John Calvin writes, "The sacraments have the same office as the Word of God," they both present Christ.[7] Yet, Calvin is equally clear that apart from the written Word of God, the sacraments are "nothing."[8] "Calvin approves of the saying of Augustine," writes Wallace, "the elements only become sacraments when the Word is added."[9] Therefore, the preaching of the Word is a necessary prerequisite to the administration of the sacraments. Calvin writes, "As soon as the sign itself meets our eyes, the Word ought to sound in our ears."[10]

When the Word of God is read, heard, and seen in the sacraments, it is a sensory experience; therefore, it is a neurological occurrence. Recalling the Word of God from memory and meditating upon it is a psychological experience. Processing the Word of God and speaking it out in praise, prayer, confession, and adoration is a psycho-neurological experience. These are experiences that every human being can engage in. But to the non-Christian, it is the condemning aroma of death; and to the Christian, it is the aroma of life. It is only when the Word of God is blessed by the Spirit that it comes alive in the soul.

It is at the act-structure level that the Spirit comes to a believer and exerts his influence on him. The Spirit enables the Christian to think God's thoughts after him and moves him to express the image of God in the world around him. It is a battle, however, that requires the Christian to utilize his neuropsychological components in order to engage with the Spirit, through the Word of God. The Spirit does not enable the Christian as a "perpetual motion machine," writes one author.[11] Rather, the Spirit is a person the Christian can cooperate with, grieve, depend upon, and respond to.[12] The Christian's relationship with the spirit is relational, and this relationship is cultivated through faith, hope, and love by the Word.

Faith, Hope and Love

At the very heart of saving faith is knowledge of God. Jesus taught that eternal life consists of the knowledge of God as revealed in and by the Word of God (John 17:3). Faith is more than the neuropsychological experience of gaining and processing information, however. After all, James said that the demons know the Word of God and tremble (James 2:19). Saving faith goes much deeper, because it gives assent to and trusts in the Word of God.[13]

> We can describe faith as our spiritual eyesight. Faith is opening our eyes to what God has done, is doing, and will do. It is living in light of these truths. It is seeing what God is like. It is seeing who we are in light of the gospel. Faith entails accepting what God says about us is true. It is trusting that he is wise, good, loving, and in control.[14]

Faith is the key that God uses to unleash the power of the Spirit and the Word in the Christian's life. Faith does not have power; it is only the instrument used to instill power. Only the Spirit along with the Word has power, and this is the very same power that raised Jesus from the dead and seated him in the heavenly places. It is a power that is at work in all who know the Christ of Scripture, give assent to his teaching, and trust him with their lives (Eph. 1:19-20).

Faith and knowledge go hand in hand, and faith and love go hand in hand as well. Faith is relational, so it is expressed outwardly as love. As one author put it,

> Love is the perfect outworking of faith. To love is to be like God. Faith and hope are to be part of our lives, but love is God's character. Love is the crown jewel, the goal of faith.[15]

When love for God and his ways are not central, Christians go astray; and if they go astray, they do not live like people of faith and hope. If this happens, true knowledge of God is distorted, assent is given to human plans, and trust is vested in the power of humans. Thus, the result is that the Spirit is grieved, his power is withdrawn, and the souls and bodies of Christians reap the consequences (cf. 1 Cor. 11:30-32). At the psychological level, Christians *will* experience a loss of love, joy, peace, and hope, and they may suffer from anger, anxiety, guilt, and depression. At the neurological level, Christians may experience restlessness, agitation, nausea, and lethargy. At the act-structure level, decisions and actions will be ungodly, hypocritical, and self-serving.

So the struggle for the Christian in the midst of illness, disease, and death concerns faith, hope, and love. The Christian must not grieve the Spirit, for the Spirit of Christ is everything to the Christian. He is life, power, and the hope of a better life to come, where there will be no more illness, disease, or death.[16]

> In this life, you have the first fruits of the Spirit; in heaven you will have the full measure. Here you see only a poor reflection; one day you will see clearly. You are heading to a place where everything is new: a new life, a new home, and a new world. This new life will have no death, pain, sorrow, or infirmities. Everything and everyone you see will be beautiful. . . . Everything you think will be pure, noble, admirable, lovely, excellent, and praiseworthy. Nothing will hinder your relationship with Jesus . . . You will not desire anything that you do not have—for all things will be yours. Your desires will be like Jesus' desires. You will be what you were created to be. You will have no fear or anxiety . . . Everything you say or sing you will mean it from the depths of your being . . . you will never again doubt the great love of God for you.[17]

The purpose of the redeeming work of Christ and the Spirit is to bring about this hope through the rebirth of a new humanity, one individual at a time, and to usher the hopeful Christian into a state of glory (cf. Rom. 1:21-22; 3:23). Sinclair Ferguson writes, "The task of the Spirit may be stated simply: to bring us to glory, to create glory within us, and to glorify us together with Christ."[18] Is it any wonder Christians suffer, since Christ's glory was in his suffering?[19] In the present state, the process of glorification has begun, and it is the end of this process that motivates hope even in the midst of suffering. Paul writes in 2 Corinthians 3:17-18:

> Now the Lord is the Spirit, and where the Spirit of the Lord is, there is freedom. And we, who with unveiled faces all reflect the Lord's glory, are being transformed into his likeness with ever-increasing glory, which comes from the Lord, who is the Spirit.

Through the new birth, the body and soul are freed by the Spirit from bondage to evil. Now a process of spiritual renewal begins in the whole human person. Outwardly our material bodies "are wasting away," writes Paul, yet inwardly our immaterial souls "are being renewed day by day" (2 Cor. 4:16). Illness, disease, trauma, decay, death, and all the evils of this world will take their inevitable toll on all Christians; but the Christian can take heart, because inwardly he or she is being renewed day by day in faith, hope, and love. Under the influence of the Holy Spirit and the Word of God on the soul, the body is now in a position to function as God originally created it, namely, to manifest the *imago Dei*. The re-creative work of the Word of God and the Spirit in the body and soul moves the believer toward one desire—renewal into the image of God. This is the all-encompassing passion and ever-growing affection of every single Christian.

The consummation of glorification will come when Jesus returns and the bodies and souls of Christians will be completely glorified. On that great day, the Christian will possess a spiritual body like that of the resurrected Christ. The full realization of the Spirit will be realized fully! In the glorified state, "The energies of God the Spirit are fully released in the resurrection body; those who possess it, consequently, experience the end of the inertia and lethargy of the flesh and an ease in serving God to the full capacity of their being."[20] Until that day, all those who possess the first-fruits "of the Spirit, groan inwardly," and wait eagerly for Christ to return and for the perfected union of their glorified bodies and souls (Rom. 8:21).

Counseling Christians in the Midst of Illness and Disease

There is perhaps no area of pastoral care more prone to misstep than ministry to those who are ill and afflicted with disease. Some of the most frequent pitfalls for a pastor are personal insecurity in dealing with illness, disease, and death; making personal experiences normative; sentimentality; working from personal rather than biblical presuppositions; rigidly applying certain protocols from counseling books; not understanding the relationship between what is considered subjective and objective data in medicine; playing doctor; providing people with reasons to avoid personal responsibility; not looking at people holistically, as body-and-soul units; refusing to accept the need for medications, particularly psychotropic drugs; being intimidated by the medical community; and not becoming a part of the healthcare team. These are but a few of the errors the pastor must be on guard against.

Approaches

How should a pastor counsel a person facing illness and disease? First and foremost, a pastor must discern to the best of his ability whether or not that person is a believer. If a person is not a Christian, then the goal of counseling must be evangelism. Illness, disease, and impending death are excellent evangelistic tools, so don't pass them up! A simple question like "What is going to help you through this?" will usually open up the conversation and provide an opportunity for a pastor to communicate a few biblical truths. It is important to pray for these people and follow up with them. The pastor needs to remember that every bit of gospel truth, in both word and deed, is used by the Holy Spirit to reveal Christ.[21]

When working with Christians facing illness and disease, the pastor will be able to counsel biblically. Initially, he must gather accurate data. First, he must find out how the condition was diagnosed.[22] Second, he needs to inquire about the history of the condition. Third, he has to discover the effects of the condition on the person's lifestyle. Fourth, he has to determine how the condition impacts the person's thinking and attitudes. Fifth, he will need to find out how relatives and friends respond to the person's condition. Sixth, he should learn about any medications that may have been prescribed.[23] The purpose of gathering data is not to verify or disprove a diagnosis but to help the pastor counsel appropriately.

Biblical Counseling and Medications

Pastors usually will be found in one of three camps when it comes to medications. In the first camp are those pastors who believe that all medications are bad, particularly psychotropic drugs. In the second camp are those who ignore medications altogether, assuming that every prescribed medication is necessary. In the third camp are pastors who understand that medications are indicated at times but also realize that they may be prescribed unnecessarily and abused by the people who use them.

The Bible clearly affirms the use of medications. In the story of the Good Samaritan (Luke 10:25-37), a mild antiseptic was used to clean the wounds of the victim. Jesus used spit, clay, and a washing in the pool of Siloam to heal a blind man (John 9:1-7).[24] Paul told Timothy to use an elixir for an abdominal ailment (1 Tim. 5:23). In the Old and New Testaments, a variety of concoctions were used for medical problems (cf. Isa. 38:21). The Levites, the public health officials, prescribed treatments for a variety of diseases (Lev. 12–13). In the Psalms, the depressed man is encouraged to experience the effects of wine in order to feel uplifted (Ps. 104:15). The writer of Proverbs advocates the amelioration of suffering through the use of alcohol, which contains ethanol, the basic chemical compound used in anesthesia (Prov. 31:6). The Bible has no qualms about medications, even medications that affect the mind; but it does take issue with abusing medications, which is idolatry, and that is one area where pastoral counseling plays an important role.

We already established the intricate unity of the body and soul and discussed the need to treat bodily problems with medications in order to address problems of the soul. The reverse is also true. Sometimes the pastor will need to treat problems of the soul in order to address problems of the body. Psychotropic medications may be helpful in this area, but if the Christian becomes dependent on the medication rather than God, the drug is being abused. The medication should help the Christian become more dependent upon God, not the medication itself. In fact, the goal in using all medications, whether they are diabetic agents, cardiac medications, narcotics, antidepressants, etc. is to maintain the homeostatic relationship of the body and soul in order to facilitate the reception of the Word of God, through faith, hope, and love, and to cultivate the Christian's relationship to the indwelling Spirit. Anything less than this is to facilitate a form of idolatry, with or without mediations. The goal of all biblical counseling is to direct the Christian to commitment and devotion to God.

The Cornerstone of Biblical Counseling
- Maintain the homeostatic balance between the body and soul, which will require assessing: (a) if a medication is needed (b) if medication is not needed.[25] A pastor will not be able to counsel effectively if this homeostatic balance is not achieved at some level.
- The reception of the Word of God through the means of grace.
- Constantly intertwine the triad of faith, hope, and love by applying the Word of God.
- Cultivate the Christian's relationship with the indwelling Spirit by encouraging self-denial, prayer, and meditation in accordance with the Word of God.

The pastor also should seek to cover the following topics when counseling, though not necessarily in this order. First, the afflicted member will need to understand how non-Christian health practitioners view illness, disease, and death so that he will not be confused by the presuppositions of Western medicine. Second, the member must be taught a biblical understanding of illness, disease, and death. He needs to hear that the ultimate cause of afflictions is sin, not blind, random processes. He also needs to know that his affliction is according to God's incomprehensible plan and that God is still in control, no matter how he feels. Third, the member must be reminded that Jesus bore all of his afflictions, no matter how ill or diseased he may become. The member needs to understand that at present God is using this affliction to sanctify him and to direct his eyes to Christ in deeper faith, hope, and love. Fourth, the member must come to terms with the fact that this affliction is beneficial in some way. God is using it for his purposes, so it is up to him and not medical science to remove it, although he may use medical techniques to do so. Fifth, the member must seek to promote good health as a steward, even if it means turning away from medical procedures that may cure the disease but destroy the body.

In counseling, the pastor should seek to discern, to the best of his ability, when medical intervention is advantageous and when it is futile, and he should know how to counsel biblically in either case. If medical intervention is advantageous, the pastor's counseling will be directed toward recovery. But if medical intervention is futile, his counseling will be directed toward comfort and accepting death.[26] It is important for the pastor to know that medical science has, in some cases, created extensive suffering, pain, psychological distress, fruitless hope, disfigurement, and immobility for many people in sincere but biased attempts to eradicate illness, disease, and syndromes at all costs. The goal of bodily stewardship, and not the healing of the body, must always be in the forefront of a pastor's thinking. Death is sometimes a welcome option for the Christian, especially if the future will be filled with extreme pain, sickness, bodily disfigurement, family distress, hopeless grasping after cures, suffering, misery, and increased expense due to protracted medical intervention.[27]

It is important for the pastor to understand the unified relationship of the body and the soul. In order for biblical counseling to be effective, it will be necessary to maintain the homeostatic relationship between the body and soul. The pastor's goal is to facilitate an atmosphere in the member's body that enables the reception of the Word of God in faith, hope, and love and to cultivate the member's relationship with the Holy Spirit. It will be necessary at times to utilize medications to do this, while at other times medications may not be needed and perhaps are actually being abused. Rooting out idolatry and encouraging dependence on God is the goal of *all* biblical counseling. One of the greatest idols Christians face today is Western medicine, with its accolades of health, wellness, and life. The pastor will have an important, difficult, and weighty role in helping his members make medical decisions that are biblically oriented.

Four

Making Decisions Regarding Medical Care

In order to approach medical decisions biblically, it will be necessary to look at the purpose of Jesus' ministry on earth and his example and teaching about sickness. In Luke 4:16-19 Jesus reveals the purpose of his mission by quoting Isaiah:

> The Spirit of the Lord is on me, because he has anointed me to preach good news to the poor. He has sent me to proclaim freedom for the prisoners and recovery of sight for the blind, to release the oppressed, to proclaim the year of the Lord's favor.

The earthly mission of Jesus was twofold: he came to preach and to heal. Jesus inaugurated a process of renewal on earth, through his preaching of repentance and his healing of mankind.

There is a third aspect to Jesus' mission that was not revealed at the synagogue in Nazareth. Jesus stopped reading the passage from Isaiah in mid-sentence. The prophecy goes on to say that Jesus also will proclaim "the day of vengeance of our God" (Isa. 61:2). Jesus was careful to distinguish between these two aspects of his overall mission. The "day of vengeance" refers to his second coming, a time that has yet to arrive and an era that is distinct from his incarnation. On the day of his second coming, Satan will be cast into hell, and all of mankind will stand before Jesus in resurrected bodies united with their souls, and he will judge them (Rev. 20:11-15). He will condemn those who rejected him, and he will acquit those who believed in him. Then after the judgment has been meted out, he will bring to completion the process of healing and renewal that was started on the earth during his incarnation.

Jesus, by his incarnation, provided a *way* for restoration from evil, illness, disease, and death in the here and now. In Mark 2:1-12 we find one of the clearest examples of what this restoration means.[1] In this episode Jesus was teaching at Peter's home in Capernaum, and the house was packed. Four men, carrying a paralytic on a cheap mattress, attempted to push their way into Peter's house to see Jesus, but they were unsuccessful. So they changed plans, and the determined men ascended a stairway on the outside of the house, with the mat and paralytic in hand. After they climbed onto the roof, they found the area above Jesus and dug a hole in the straw and clay roof. After they broke through the roof and widened the hole, they lowered the paralytic to Jesus. Mark writes:

When Jesus saw their faith, he said to the paralytic, "Son, your sins are forgiven." Now some teachers of the law were sitting there, thinking to themselves, "Why does this fellow talk like that? He's blaspheming! Who can forgive sins but God alone?" Immediately Jesus knew in his spirit that this was what they were thinking in their hearts, and he said to them, "Why are you thinking these things? Which is easier: to say to the paralytic, 'Your sins are forgiven,' or to say, 'Get up, take your mat and walk'? But that you may know that the Son of Man has authority on earth to forgive sins. . . ." He said to the paralytic, "I tell you, get up, take your mat and go home." He got up, took his mat and walked out in full view of them all.

The first thing to notice in this passage is that Jesus responded to the "faith" of the men. The men believed that Jesus had the authority and power to restore the paralytic, so they were determined to bring the paralytic to him. Second, Jesus initially did not heal the paralytic physically but instead forgave his sins. In so doing Jesus teaches that a priority exists. The man's spiritual, or moral, condition takes precedence over his physical condition. Third, Jesus provided physical healing, not for the sake of healing the man, but in order to testify of his authority to forgive sins and to show that he possessed the power to grant a full future restoration.

In fact, every act of physical healing, exorcism, or resurrection performed by Jesus was focused on his authority and his power to restore, and not on the act itself. Illness, disease, and death exist to accomplish God's purposes and to bring forth glory to Jesus. John 9:1-3 records an episode in which the disciples asked Jesus about a man who was born blind.

"Rabbi, who sinned, this man or his parents, that he was born blind?" "Neither this man nor his parents sinned," said Jesus, "but this happened so that the work of God might be displayed in his life."

Jesus taught that the man was born blind, not because of any directly related sin, as the disciples thought, but "that the work of God might be displayed in his life."[2] In another passage John writes,

When he heard [that Lazarus was sick], Jesus said, "This sickness will not end in death. No, it is for God's glory so that God's Son may be glorified through it." (11:4).

In both of these passages, we read that Jesus is glorified by demonstrating his authority over sin, evil, illness, disease, and death, and by his power a process of reversal and true healing begins that will lead ultimately to the full restoration of the entire creation.

The reality is that even though Jesus healed people, cast out demons, and resurrected the dead, all these same people still suffered illness, disease, and trauma; thus, they all died one day. So, was the restorative work of Jesus ineffective? God forbid, no! By these acts of healing, Jesus was testifying to his authority and power. He was showing the world that he is the only one who can truly fix mankind's problem and provide the necessary healing that endures. It is in this context that decisions regarding medical treatment need to be made.

Healing or HEALING!

Certainly, it is not wrong to pray for or believe in healing miracles; nor is it wrong to seek medical treatment. If it is God's will to miraculously heal a person, then he will do so. If it is God's will to heal a person through medical intervention, then he will do this as well. It is *always* wrong, however, to seek healing miracles and medical treatments for the sake of healing. Simply stated, it may not be God's will for a person to be healed. If this is the case, seeking medical treatment and healing miracles may lead to idolatry, hopelessness, spiritual anguish, psychological distress, increased pain, misery, suffering, financial problems, social turmoil, and dependency on others.

Jesus taught us that evil is the main problem humans have to contend with, not illness, disease, and death. These are the result of evil. Jesus' primary purpose in his incarnation was to send a message and not to heal mankind physically. Now that his testimonial record has been established and the closing of the canon of Scripture has occurred, healings are no longer necessary. He has already testified to his authority and power, and now this testimony is found in the pages of Holy Scripture. It is wonderful to see a sick sister healed physically, whether by miracle or medical treatment, but it is equally praiseworthy to see her persevere under affliction and die in her Lord with no medical treatment. In both instances, the main problem of evil has been dealt with, and the testimony of God's written record has been stamped upon her life.

The Bible teaches that God uses affliction to test Christians. Through the experience of suffering and misery, Christians become more dependent upon God and not on mankind. It is during times of sickness that we are more apt to cry out to God and to seek his help more diligently. In the midst of the fiery furnace of pain, anguish, and torment, the believer is purged of self-reliance and made to rely more on God (2 Cor. 3:18). God is sovereign, and he is a caring and proud Father who loves to draw his children closer to him. He brings illness, suffering, trauma, disease, and death into the lives of Christians for his, and their, good purposes.

The Goals of God in Affliction

Afflictions, and all the suffering that goes along with them, are universal to all of mankind, and they are used by God to accomplish his goals. One of God's goals is to drive people to seek the hope of restoration found only in Christ. To the non-Christian, illness, disease, and death are but a gentle foretaste of the eternal torments reserved for those who are without Christ (Matt. 25:41). In his grace, God brings affliction into the lives of non-Christians in order to reveal to them their need for him. All too often, however, non-Christians curse God for their afflictions rather than turn to him for help and restoration. And there are times when a non-Christian will seek God but when the affliction has been removed forget about him. Non-Christians refuse to submit to their Creator and acknowledge their need for his forgiveness (Rom. 1:20-23). Therefore, God condemns them to hell when they die.

A second goal is to warn (Deut. 28:58ff.). Afflictions are used to warn people of ungodly living. Both the Christian and non-Christian can suffer from certain illnesses and diseases because of profane living. For example, the alcoholic who suffers from cirrhosis of the liver does so because of ungodly living. Alcoholics Anonymous has affirmed this biblical truth for many years. In the AA *Big Book* we read,

> So our troubles, we think, are basically of our own making. They arise out of ourselves, and the alcoholic is an extreme example of self-will run riot, though he usually doesn't think so. Above everything, we alcoholics must be rid of this selfishness. We must, or it kills us! God makes that possible.[3]

At the heart of alcoholism are "self-will run riot" and "selfishness." In Christian lingo, this is called sin and ungodliness. So, technically speaking, alcoholism is not a disease; but it can be a precursor to other diseases such as cirrhosis of the liver. God will use the effects of alcohol abuse and other acts of self-indulgent behavior to alert Christians and non-Christians to self-centered living and of their need for repentance.

A third goal is to sanctify Christians (Rom. 8:28–29). The Christian is sanctified by God's providential hand in the experience of sickness, infectious diseases, congenital

defects, and dying. First, a Christian who suffers these afflictions will enter into the experience of Christ and become
more like him in suffering (Rom. 8:29). Second, illness,
disease, and death are reminders of the fleeting nature of this
life and the hope of eternal rest to come (James 4:14; Rom.
8:18). Third, endurance under misery and suffering testifies
to a Christian's character and to God's sustaining grace (Job
2:3–6; 1 Cor. 10:13). Fourth, affliction, sickness, disease, and
impending death are used to *increase* a believer's ministry.[4]
The Christian who sees the providential hand of God behind
his afflictions as a means of sanctification will find great
comfort in knowing that God is in control. "God never lays
a rod upon his children's back," writes William Bridge, "but
he first puts a staff into their hand to bear it."[5]

Sickness, illness, infections, and the dying process, with
all of their attendant misery, prepare Christians for everlasting
wellness, health, and life in their eternal rest to come (Rev.
21:4). Richard Baxter (1615-1691), in his book *The Saint's
Everlasting Rest,* provides insight into how God prepares
Christians for eternal life. Baxter knew the afflicting hand
of God well. He wrote the book while he was suffering from
chronic pain and tuberculosis and was near death. During
this time he looked death in the face, and according to his
testimony he experienced the sufficient grace of God. Baxter
was spared from death at this time, but the remnants of the
disease and the chronic pain he suffered plagued him until he
entered his everlasting rest in 1691.

Baxter seeks to impress upon the reader that the Christian
should expect pain, suffering, distress, sickness, disease, and
death in this present life. It is through affliction that God
transforms the Christian into his glorious image. He says
that affliction reminds the Christian that rest should not
be sought in this world. It is only after much suffering, he
writes, that the Christian's rest will be its sweetest. Besides,
who would desire a heavenly rest if a sweet rest was found in

this present life? "Afflictions speak convincingly and will be heard when preachers cannot," writes Baxter.[6] He goes on to say that when a man is "fastened to his bed with pining sickness, the world is nothing, and heaven is something."[7]

> Many thousand recovered sinners may cry, "O healthful sickness! O comfortable sorrows! O gainful losses! O enriching poverty! O blessed day that ever I was afflicted!" Not only the "green pastures and still waters, but the rod and staff, they comfort us." Though the word and Spirit do the main work, yet suffering so unbolts the door of the heart, that his word has an easier entrance.[8]

It is also in the midst of illness, disease, and death that the idols of our hearts are dealt with. Often Christians do not see health, wellness, and life as idols, but they can be. When a sickness strikes, most Christians will think of how to get better first and seek God second. Christians are commanded to worship the God of health, wellness, and life, not health, wellness, and life themselves. In fact, to turn to a physician without turning to God first is rank idolatry (cf. 2 Kings 1; 2 Chron. 16:12). The Christian must remember that God alone is the source of all health, wellness, and life, and he must be acknowledged as such (Exod. 15:26; Job 5:18). In the midst of sickness, affliction, illness, disease, and even death, what we worship will be exposed. Is it health, wellness, or life, or is it God?

Paul's life testimony was, "To live is Christ, and to die is gain" (Phil. 1:21). In America's Christianity, this kind of commitment is nearly nonexistent. Paul's testimony, however, should be the norm, not the exception. So what is behind a Christian's unwillingness to leave this world and to be with the Lord forever? Baxter suggests four things. First is the Christian's infidelity to God. Baxter asks whether it is possible for a Christian to believe that death will alleviate his misery and usher him into glory and yet not desire to die. Second is the Christian's coldness of love for God. Here Baxter says that if we love our friend, we will love his company. If a Christian loves God warmly, wouldn't he want to be close to him? Third is the Christian's lack of weariness of sin. Baxter asks the Christian, "Do you suffer from separation anxiety from the world?" Fourth is the Christian's desensitization to the world.

> O unworthy soul would you rather dwell in this land of darkness and wander in this barren wilderness, than be at rest with Jesus Christ? Who would rather stay among the wolves and daily suffer the scorpion's stings, than praise the Lord with the host of heaven . . . This unwillingness to die actually convicts us of high treason against the Lord! Isn't this a choosing the world before him? Isn't this delighting in things present for our happiness? Don't these things become our gods if we do not desire to be with the Lord?[9]

I would add a fifth reason Christians do not desire to leave this world, one that Baxter does not speak about, and that is the felt need to provide for others. It sounds admirable, but Jesus taught that Christians should always be ready to die and to trust God to provide for those left behind (Luke 12:12; 7:11).

This present life is a time of sanctification, which means death: death to self, death to the world, death to sin, death to Satan, death to wellness, death to health, and death to life. But it also means life to the everlasting God, who is the author of all life. It is through affliction that the process of sanctification is made possible, as Baxter notes. The saint shall never find rest in this present life, and to seek it here is idolatry! The ultimate and overarching goal of all illness, disease, and death is to bring glory to God, whether through judgment, affliction, restoration, or endurance. It is important for a sick Christian to remember this truth, so that no matter how sick or debilitated he may become, God is still working out his purposes in him, and his death will be great gain (cf. Phil. 1:9).

So, in a temporal and eschatological sense, illness, disease, and death are always beneficial, though not necessarily pleasant to the Christian. Christians truly believe "that *all* things work together for their good" (Rom. 8:28, emphasis mine). This means, as Dr. Robert Smith comments in *The Christian Counselor's Medical Desk Reference,* that getting "over the illness should *not* be the primary goal" for a Christian.

> What glorifies [God] is what is best for all believers; therefore what glorifies Him will be the best for the sick believer. Getting well is not necessarily the best thing. . . . The hope for the believer is victory, not relief. Relief is not inherently wrong, but it becomes wrong when it is the primary goal. God promises victory *in* illnesses and trials, not deliverance *from* them.[10]

This distinction is very important, especially in light of the advancements in modern medicine.

The Christian's Use of Modern Medicine

If the providence of God is behind illness, disease, and death and these afflictions benefit the Christian, why seek medical treatment at all? The reason is that Christians must be good stewards of their bodies and souls. There is an important categorical difference at this point. Christians do not seek medical treatment simply in order to get well; rather, Christians seek wellness and health in order to take care of their bodies and to maintain the homeostatic relationship between the body and soul (1 Cor. 6:19–20). If the possibility exists for a Christian to improve his health, then he should do so, "that [he] may continue serving the Lord as long and as productively as possible."[11]

By the same token, a Christian can be a poor steward of her body when she seeks medical treatment that will destroy her body and impair the homeostatic relationship between the body and soul. I am reminded of a dear Christian woman who received chemotherapy and radiation treatment for cancer. She suffered more from the treatment, the complications to her body, and the aftermath of spiritual suffering than from the disease itself. Aside from the destructive side effects during the initial treatment, months later she developed excruciating pain in her mouth area, the location of the radiation treatments. Her teeth and jaw became painfully brittle and even started to rot. In an attempt to alleviate the pain, she became addicted to the pain medication and physically dependent upon it and was frequently constipated as a result of it. Eventually, she became embittered, critical of those around her, and depressed; and due to her inability to eat, she was emaciated, weighed about eighty pounds. She was bed bound most of the time, and her lack of mobility caused a decrease in bone density, which resulted in fractures, muscular atrophy, and painful bedsores. If this weren't enough, the poor woman contracted agonizing shingles on her abdominal area. The cancer was eradicated, but her body was destroyed, and her soul suffered the consequences. This woman lived another two years in this awful state before she died.

Thus, the ongoing progress in medical science poses difficult challenges for Christians. Medical science has provided many welcomed advances, but it also has created some profound moral and ethical dilemmas. Less than seventy years ago, the options for treatment of the critically ill were limited, and consequently so were a patient's options. Now, with the considerable advances in medical and technological treatments, such as cardiopulmonary resuscitation, respirators, kidney dialysis, organ transplants, surgical procedures, antibiotics, cancer chemotherapy and radiation, intravenous nourishment, and feeding tubes, a seriously ill person, who probably would have died years earlier can be kept alive. This increasing ability to preserve life raises perplexing questions for Christians and the pastors who counsel them.

In order to help the Christian navigate the sea of modern medicine, answering four questions will be very helpful. The first question was already mentioned, namely, how will this medical treatment help the Christian be a good steward of his body? In other words, will this treatment help the body or not? Second, how is this treatment going to assist the Christian in advancing the kingdom of God on earth (Matt. 6:33)? It may be necessary for a Christian to endure the suffering caused by a medical, surgical, or a pharmaceutical treatment in order to get well and serve God and others in the future. Third, will this treatment destroy the body and have the potential to fail in the end anyway (Ps. 38:15)? Fourth, does this treatment have the potential of making the person a long-term burden on others?[12] An answer for most illnesses and diseases will be found after answering the first two questions. But the more complicated conditions, such as cancer, organ failure, congenital anomalies, etc. will require answers to questions 3 and 4 also. So when answering questions 3 and 4, it will be important to gather all the diagnostic and prognostic information possible.

Summary of Questions to Consider
1. How will this medical treatment help the Christian be a good steward of his or her body?
2. How is this treatment going to assist the Christian in advancing the kingdom of God on earth?

3. Will this treatment destroy the body and have the potential to fail in the end anyway?
4. Does this treatment have the potential of making the Christian a long-term burden on others?

Case Study: Steve

Steve was married with four children. About a month ago he was diagnosed with prostate cancer with metastasis to his pelvis. After all the diagnostic tests were performed, the cancer was found to be aggressive, and he was given a prognosis of less than six months to live. The medical team recommended treating the cancer with a radical surgery, chemotherapy, and radiation treatment. Steve asked himself questions 1 and 2: "Will this treatment help me be a good steward of my body, and how is this treatment going to assist me in advancing the kingdom of God on earth?" He answered, "My body will suffer greatly, but I need to provide for my family. If the treatment works, I will be able to do so." Steve was keenly aware of his poor prognosis, however. Questions 3 and 4 were important to answer as well. After gathering all the information possible and obtaining a second opinion, Steve, his wife, and their pastor prayerfully pondered these two questions together. According to both oncologists, the surgery, chemotherapy, and radiation would have a 30 percent chance of success, and the immediate and long-term side effects would be debilitating. After weighing all the data, both biblical and medical, it was decided that treatment would not be the best option. Steve did not want to be a long-term burden to his family, and he would be able to provide for his family through the collection of his life insurance policy after he died. Steve and his wife, with the pastor's help, made the difficult decision to forego the treatment. Steve went on to live for six months before he died.

Case Study: Suzy

Suzy was a fifty-five-year-old single missionary to Sudan. One day, while she was riding her bike between villages, she experienced shortness of breath and chest pain. She was evacuated by the mission team to a city hospital. At the hospital she was diagnosed with coronary artery disease. Her diagnostic tests revealed blockages in three of her arteries, and open-heart surgery was required. Suzy pondered questions 1 and 2. Her answer was, "The surgery will improve circulation to my heart, and I will be able to continue my mission work to the Sudanese." After reflecting on the seriousness of the condition, she decided to sit down with her pastor, and together they considered questions 3 and 4. Bypass surgery is a routine procedure with a 90 percent chance of success, and even greater for someone with Suzy's good health. Suzy would be incapacitated and dependent upon others for at least three months, but she would most likely experience a full recovery. Suzy and her pastor decided that surgery would be the best option. After six months, Suzy returned to the mission field with slightly limited activity and on a prescribed blood thinner and heart pill. Suzy entered into her rest many years later on the Sudan mission field at the age of eighty-five.

Case Study: Freddy

Steve and Suzy were able to make decisions by themselves, but what about those difficult cases where a person cannot speak on his own behalf? What about a loved one on life support? Freddy was a seven-year-old boy who had sustained an anoxic brain injury due to a drowning accident while on visitation with his father. He was resuscitated but remained in a coma. He continued in this comatose state, connected to life support and a feeding tube for six weeks. The doctors asked Freddy's mother, his custodial parent, if she desired to wean him off the artificial life support since his potential for recovery looked poor. Freddy's mother, in consultation with her pastor, made the difficult decision to remove the life-support apparatus. After doing so, Freddy did not die. His heart and lungs functioned independently. A later neurological exam and electroencephalogram (EEG) revealed that Freddy had no brain activity. The doctors said that Freddy had irreversible brain damage and that he was in a persistent vegetative state (PVS).

Although his heart, lungs, and brain stem were all functioning to sustain his life, Freddy could not care for himself, and he had little to no chance of recovery. This led to other difficult questions for Freddy's mother and pastor. What about the feeding tube? What about aggressive treatment in the future to sustain Freddy's life? The two prayerfully pondered the questions mentioned above. It was decided that God owns Freddy's life and that for some reason when the life support was removed, he allowed Freddy's heart to pump and his lungs to breath. Therefore, Freddy's mother had the ethical and moral obligation to feed her son, even if it was through a feeding tube. They also decided that no aggressive medical treatment would be sought in the future. If Freddy took a turn for the worse, she would keep him comfortable and let him die. Although Freddy was extremely difficult to care for, the church was able to help, and this had a catalyzing effect on everyone who came into contact with him.

Each individual case the pastor encounters will be unique, and each one must be considered on its own merits. There are no patented answers when it comes to dealing with the morals and ethics of complex medical decisions. However, when the Christian is required to navigate the sea of modern medicine, certain fundamental principles must govern his thought. The pastor, as well, must keep the following principles in the forefront of his mind when counseling.

First, the Christian has been healed already. No matter how sick, diseased, or debilitated the Christian becomes, he is still in Christ. Second, God in his providence uses illness, disease, and death to sanctify Christians. These afflictions are always beneficial to the Christian in some way, and they are always meaningful. Therefore, third, a great deal of biblical wisdom is required when making medical decisions. The goal for the Christian is not healing but God's glory. Sometimes the Christian will require healing in order to serve God on earth, but at other times, the Christian may be called to complete HEALING in heaven (cf. Rev. 21:1–4).

Summary of Principles when Christians Engage Western Medicine

1. No matter how sick, diseased, or debilitated a Christian becomes, he is still in Christ; therefore he is healed already.
2. God in his providence uses illness, disease, and death to sanctify Christians.
3. The goal for the Christian is not healing but God's glory; for this reason, a great deal of biblical wisdom is required when making medical decisions.

The Pastor and Advance Directives

The pastor can assist his congregation immensely and provide a framework for future counseling by discussing advanced directives.[13] An advance directive describes the type of medical care a person would like to have in the event that he cannot speak for himself due to an illness, disease, or traumatic injury. Discussing advance directives not only plans ahead, but it also helps the pastor to counsel biblically. Laws for advance directives vary from state to state, but the three main documents are a living will, durable healthcare power of attorney, and a do-not-resuscitate order (DNR).[14]

A living will is a written, legal document that describes specifically the kind of medical or life-sustaining treatments desired if a person becomes seriously or terminally ill. It defines a person's wishes, and it will assist others in making medical decisions on behalf of the person who cannot speak for himself. A second advance directive is a durable healthcare power of attorney. A durable healthcare power of attorney is a legal document that identifies a person chosen to make medical decisions on another person's behalf, and it should be used in conjunction with a living will. The document becomes active anytime a person is unconscious or unable to make medical decisions. A third advance directive is a "do-not-resuscitate order" (DNR). A DNR is a written document that states that a person does not want cardiopulmonary resuscitation (CPR) if his heart stops beating or if he stops breathing. Any person who is eighteen years of age or older can prepare advance directives.

Advance directives are an effective way for the pastor to assist his members in making clear and informed medical decisions about present and future medical care. As mentioned earlier, the directives will help the pastor counsel his members biblically and provide guidance when medical crises arise. The documents are easy to prepare, but they may need to be notarized and will have to follow any unique regulations of a specific state. Advance directives can be changed and rewritten at any time, provided the person is of a sound mind, but if they are changed, they will need to be notarized once again and redistributed to all the involved parties. It is important to destroy all old copies of advance directives if they are rewritten.

The pastor plays an important role in helping his members engage Western medicine in light of God's providence and will and in assisting them in making informed biblical decisions concerning their medical care. Advance directives will help the pastor know his congregation better, and they will assist him in future counseling on his member's behalf concerning difficult medical decisions. The pastor will need to be especially skilled, however, in helping members after they have made the decision to forego curative medical treatment and have decided to let their disease run its course.

Five

Pastoral Care and Counseling at End of Life

Within the last forty years, hospice and palliative care services have gained a reputable position in the medical community. This was due mostly to the pioneering work of Elisabeth Kübler-Ross (1926-2004), who in 1969 published *On Death and Dying*, a scathing indictment of the medical community's ignorance, insensitivity, fear, and approach to death and dying. In the words of *Time* magazine, Dr. Kübler-Ross "has brought death out of the darkness." Not long after Kübler-Ross's book came out, federal legislation facilitated a hospice benefit for Medicare, and private insurers followed suit. This benefit is now available to people over sixty-five with a prognosis of six months or less to live. As a result, hospice agencies sprouted throughout the United States.

The goal of hospice care is not to cure the disease but to reduce the symptoms of the disease by providing physical, emotional, and spiritual support to the patient and family. This means that treatment is palliative in nature and does not include such measures as cardiopulmonary resuscitation or other advanced life-support systems. The person signing onto the hospice program agrees to forego any further medical treatment for his or her disease and is making a decision to have death come without further medical intervention, whereas, the goal of conventional medicine is to cure the disease at all costs. It is very important for the pastor to understand this distinction and to make sure that the patient and his or her family understand it well. Hospice means no more curative treatment.

"Death: The Final Stage of Growth"

I mentioned earlier that it was important for the pastor to become part of the hospice team; now I will go into greater detail to explain why. I also said earlier that it is impossible to have a philosophical system totally confined to the physical universe, which is what naturalism tries to do. We saw that in response to this problem the medical community developed a type of New Age spirituality. Dr. Kübler-Ross was a pioneer in this New Age movement as well, and it is her views on death and the afterlife that reflect the majority consensus in Western medical thought today. Kübler-Ross believed that death was the final state of evolutionary growth, and it gave birth to a mysterious new stage of life—an afterlife that is always full of bliss and in harmony with one's personal beliefs.

One does not have to study Kübler-Ross long to see her focus on the unconscious interior world that Freud, Jung, and Maslow espoused. For Kübler-Ross, however, the union between the conscious and unconscious, the self-actualized state, was a state achieved through death. In her 1975 edition of *Death: The Final Stage of Growth,* she writes, "I hope to convey one important message to my readers: namely, that death does not have to be a catastrophic, destructive thing; indeed, it can be viewed as one of the most constructive, positive, and creative elements of culture and life."[1] Death for Kübler-Ross is the doorway to the unconscious interior world of true being and the pinnacle of evolutionary growth.

The "Five Stages of Grief" is the work that Kübler-Ross is best known for, and most hospice programs recognize her paradigm as valid. According to Kübler-Ross in her book on *Death and Dying*, it is the goal of the clinician to identify these various stages and to assist the patient comfortably through them, while at the same time maintaining a hope for the possibility of healing. For Kübler-Ross, reality does not matter; rather feelings matter most. Thus she sees denial and hope in an "unforeseen" cure to be a means of "healthy" coping.[2]

The five stages in her model are: (1) denial and isolation, (2) anger, (3) bargaining, (4) depression, and (5) acceptance. First, according to Kübler-Ross, denial is a stage that never truly leaves the patient. As mentioned already, she sees denial as an effective means of coping and regards it "as a buffer after unexpected shocking news."[3] Isolation appears to be more consonant with her later stage of depression, so I will discuss it then. Second, anger comes about when "denial cannot be maintained any longer."[4] In this stage the patient asks the question, "Why me?" Anger occurs, according to Kübler-Ross, because the patient believes that he or she is being treated unjustly. Third is bargaining, which Kübler-Ross sees as "equally helpful to the patient," in order to cope, "though only for brief periods of time."[5] According to Kübler-Ross, in this stage the patient tries to make some sort of agreement, usually with God, in order to postpone death. Fourth is depression, which Kübler-Ross sees as preparatory for the acceptance of death. The stage of depression reflects the earlier stage of isolation, which according to Kübler-Ross is a stage of quiet, self-isolating grief.[6] Fifth is acceptance, which is a stage of resignation. In this stage the patient "will be tired and, in most cases, quite weak" and will be dozing on and off. It is not a "happy stage" but somber one, writes Kübler-Ross, and is "almost void of feelings."[7]

Analysis of Dr. Kübler-Ross's Teaching

Kübler-Ross was correct in her focus on hope, but her basis for hope was seriously flawed. The flavor of the synergism she advocates can lead only to futility and hopelessness. Kübler-Ross rejected the hope of the Bible. Instead of believing the Bible, she drew on her medical and psychiatric training and a whole host of philosophical and religious systems, and she founded a new kind of hope. She placed her faith in this self-constructed system of belief, and as a zealous devotee to her convictions she proselytized the world around her. Her unique religious system is a true opiate for the people (as Karl Marx once said of all religious systems), because it divorces a person from reality. Kübler-Ross sought to give hope with a hopeless system of denial. As a result, she asserted an illusory dogma that can never provide true hope in the face of death, not even her own death.[8]

Kübler-Ross's "Five Stages of Grief" are accurate insofar as they describe human psychology. But the idea that a progression exists is not correct, especially if a person continues to hold on to the hope that she advocates, which is ultimately a form of denial. It is more accurate to see these so-called stages as in constant flux and not as "stages" but as "states." Typically, when a person hears that he is going to die, denial does indeed set in, but it is usually in the form of an unrealistic acceptance of death! It also must be noted at this point that these stages depict normal human psychology in our fallen state. All of us experience denial and isolation, anger, bargaining, depression, and acceptance in our everyday lives. In a crisis situation, any crisis situation for that matter as defined by an individual, these stages may be accentuated, and at that point, a person may exhibit "abnormal" behavior.

Denial is never a healthy way of coping, as Kübler-Ross also suggests. It is a psychological response that exists because of mankind's fallen condition (cf. Gen. 3). In fact, all the other states—anger, bargaining, depression, isolation, and even acceptance, in Kübler-Ross's sense of the term—are not entered into after denial is dealt with but *are* the result of the psychological tension caused by denial! If a person is not in denial, then he accepts reality, and contentment is the result. All the states mentioned by Kübler-Ross are theaters of battle, where denial must be fought moment by moment with the use of the weapons of faith, hope, love, and truth. It is a daily struggle, not a progression to acceptance, especially the illusory acceptance Kübler-Ross has in mind. The Christian is a theistic realist (not a synergistic, deistic relativist), who exercises faith and love in a historical person called Jesus Christ and has the hope of a better life to come as revealed in the pages of Holy Scripture.

Death: The Final Stage of Sin

The paragraph below describes Kübler-Ross's stage of acceptance.

If a patient has had enough time (i.e., not a sudden, unexpected death) and has been given some help in working through the previously described stages, he will reach a stage during which he is neither depressed nor angry about his "fate." He will have been able to express his previous feelings, his envy for the living and the healthy and his anger at those who do not have to face their end so soon. He will have mourned the impending loss of so many meaningful people and places and he will contemplate his coming end with a certain degree of quiet expectation. He will be tired and, in most cases, quite weak. He will also have a need to doze off to sleep often and in brief intervals, which is different from the need to sleep during the times of depression.[9]

As a person nears death, some of the most common physical problems experienced are pain, nausea, vomiting, anorexia, nutritional and hydration problems, constipation, shortness of breath, urinary incontinence, and pressure sores. It is also during this time, as Kübler-Ross notes, that a person may become introverted, sleep more often, and communicate less with those around him. But is this really the enlightened psychological state of acceptance that Kübler-Ross suggests? Or is it the compulsory state of impending death imposed on the body by a body that is dying? It is more likely the latter. The person has no other option but to "accept" what is happening to him!

As the body lingers on in this state of forced decline, a person may experience increased disorientation, confusion, agitation, hallucinations, delusions, and depression, as well as a decrease in blood pressure, an increase in heart rate, a change in skin color, an increase in perspiration, respiratory irregularities and congestion, a semi-comatose state, an increase or decrease in body temperature, and a body that feels tired, weak, and heavy. Then in days to hours before death, a person may experience a short-lived sudden surge of energy, followed by a downward plummet that is characterized by an intensification of the signs and symptoms mentioned earlier. In minutes before death, a person may gasp for air, enter into a coma, have glassy and teary eyes, and cold, clammy, pale, gray, ashen, or bluish skin. Finally, the breath of life ceases, the heart stops pumping, and the eyes become dull and fixated—the person is dead.

Death due to chronic illness is seldom rapid. It is usually a slow, continuous process of decline over a period of hours, days, weeks, and months with physiological and psychological changes. During the dying process, the body is unable to cope with decreased blood oxygen, malnutrition, electrolyte imbalances, and metabolic toxins. The failing liver and kidneys are unable to filter the bodily waste products, so they build up in the blood. The accumulated metabolites will eventually affect the brain, and when the brain is affected, emotion, cognition, thinking, behavior, and autonomic nervous function are impaired. In most cases a person eventually will pass into a coma. There are two roads to a coma, notes Dr. Robert E. Enck in *The Medical Care of Terminally Ill Patients*, "the high road and the low road."

> The low road is the more common and is a path of increasing sedation to coma and death. This path does not seem to be traumatic for patients, and surviving friends and relatives generally recall a peaceful death . . . the high road is much more traumatic, resembling the organic brain syndrome of delirium.[10]

If the person is on the high road, he may experience increased restlessness, extreme confusion, hallucinations, agitation, muscular twitching, and seizures. But whether the person is on the high road or low road, death is never a pleasant process or an enlightened state of acceptance—it is always the culmination of human misery because of sin.

End-of-Life Care and Counseling

As mentioned earlier, the goal of hospice care is to alleviate suffering, not only spiritually but also mentally and physically. This is an admirable goal and should be viewed as such. Jesus alleviated mental and physical anguish everywhere he went. In order to accomplish this task, hospice agencies have several medications to assist them. There are two groups of medications the pastor must be aware of: psychotropic drugs (that treat anxiety, depression, psychosis, neuropathic pain, etc.) and narcotics (that treat visceral pain and shortness of breath). These medications concern the pastor, because they can have adverse and unwanted side effects, can be abused, and can cause an overdose. These medications are not used to hasten death but to treat symptoms. Nevertheless, the pastor needs to be observant when they are being used, because they can be idolized by the Christian, and it is often a non-Christian healthcare professional, an idolater, who is administering them.

It will be important for the pastor to establish with the dying individual, if conscious, the level of pain and discomfort he is willing to endure and, along with the patient, to communicate this to the hospice nurse.[11] The goal is to keep the member as physically and mentally comfortable as possible, while maintaining consciousness, clarity, and the ability to communicate, and not to overly sedate him.[12] The pastor should encourage the member to make his last days on earth a blessing to others through his undying testimony of God's grace to him in Jesus Christ.

The main focus of counseling for the dying Christian is to alleviate spiritual, mental, and physical suffering in order to increase devotion to God, to help the dying person and the person's family understand properly this providential affliction, and to assist them as death nears. The pastor must be aware that when the dying member nears death, significant changes will occur, not only physically, but also mentally, and medications may be used effectively to treat the symptoms that develop. The dying person may experience nausea, pain, breathlessness, depression, anxiety, mania, hallucinations, and a host of other physiological and psychological afflictions due to the crisis, spiritual malady, physical sickness, underlying psychosis, or the disease process. Psychotropic drugs and narcotics can be used effectively to *maintain* mental stability and to provide important physical comfort to the individual that will permit the pastor to counsel biblically. The pastor can assist the hospice team greatly by identifying these physical and mental afflictions and reporting them to the hospice nurse so that he or she can give the proper medications and adjust the dosages as needed.[13] Remember, the homeostasis of body and soul is crucial when counseling.

Where counseling should begin on end-of-life issues depends on how well the dying person and the person's family are coping with the impending death. No matter where the pastor begins, however, there are four hopeful teachings that he should consciously and continuously intertwine as he counsels. First and foremost, he must bring to remembrance the victory that Christ has over death (1 Cor. 15:55). Although death may be a fearful foe and dying may be miserable, Christ has gained the victory and has eliminated its sting. Death for the Christian is the doorway to Emmanuel's land and the place where mortality puts on immortality. It is the place where illness, disease, pain, suffering, and death will be completely done away with. Second, the pastor should bring assurance to the individual. It is important to communicate clearly that God accepts everyone who sincerely believes in Jesus, and he will never leave him nor forsake him (John 10:27–29; Rom. 8:31–39). Third, the pastor should address the individual's many questions: What is the providence of God in all of this (Rom. 8:28)? Why is God doing this? What will happen to my family after I am gone? How will God be glorified? Fourth, the pastor should remind the individual of the promises of eternal life to come. There are several passages a pastor can turn to in this area. Three of my favorites are John 14:1–6 and Revelation 21:1–4 and 22:1–5. At all times, the pastor must remember to pray and to sing psalms, hymns, and spiritual songs with the dying individual and his family.[14]

Summary of Four Hopeful Teachings for the Dying Christian
1. Bring to remembrance the victory that Christ has had over death.
2. Communicate clearly that Jesus will never leave nor forsake his own.
3. Address all questions biblically, even if the answers are difficult to accept.
4. Constantly point to the promises of eternal life to come.

The pastor also will have some very important social work to do, so it will be important to mobilize the diaconal team in the congregation. The family and dying member will require extensive and organized support, both during and after the death. Diaconal care may include but is not limited to organizing visitations, providing opportunities for the family to get away, providing meals, watching children, taking care of pets, and assistance around the house, etc. The pastor will need to make funeral arrangements with the dying member and family as well. This is a difficult but important and necessary step. After the member dies, the hospice nurse will pronounce him dead, and the funeral home will remove the body from the house. Making many of the funeral arrangements beforehand eliminates a great amount of unnecessary stress on the family, and planning the funeral with the dying member and the family may be a healthy experience. The pastor must recognize that he is only one part—but an important part—of the hospice team and church team, and he cannot do it all.

Finally, the pastor has the important responsibility of providing bereavement counseling for the family. Immediately following the death, the pastor should plan to visit the closest family members daily for a few days until the funeral, then weekly for four weeks, monthly for the next two months, and periodically thereafter.[15] The pastor must keep in mind that the impact of death does not usually hit the family until a month or two later. Counseling should initially focus on helping the person(s) grieve. It is not normal for family members to be insensitive to the death of a loved one; they should feel sadness and grief. If this is not obvious to the pastor, he should ask whether or not the person(s) has cried over the death. Helping to process the death, understanding the death biblically, and moving on in fervent service for Christ will be the primary goals of the pastor in bereavement counseling.[16]

Case Study: Ruth

Ruth was a twenty-three-year-old single Christian woman who was diagnosed with terminal breast cancer with metastasis throughout her body. About four weeks prior to her diagnosis, Ruth saw her primary care physician for increasing pain in her breasts and back and periodic episodes of shortness of breath. After the exam, her primary care doctor sent Ruth for a mammogram. The mammogram revealed several tumors in her breasts, and a later full body MRI revealed metastasis throughout her entire body. Ruth received diagnostic and prognostic confirmation from two oncologists, and they both told Ruth that she had less than two months to live, so she was referred to hospice services.

Almost immediately, due to the excruciating pain and shocking news, Ruth went into a state of depression. She had dull, achy pain all over her body but particularly in her back. Ruth's mood was flat, and she complained of feeling "numb." Ruth stayed in bed most of the time, wanted to be left alone, and ate next to nothing. The hospice nurse recommended to the doctor that she start Decadron, Ritalin, and MS Contin. The doctor agreed and ordered the medications. Decadron is a steroid that decreases pain caused by systemic inflammation and increases the appetite. Ritalin is a stimulant that helps to elevate the mood in the adult population. MS Contin is a long-acting narcotic that controls pain by acting on the brain. After two days of taking the drugs, Ruth's mood was elevated, her appetite was better, her energy level was increased, and she was nearly pain free. The side effects from the medication were minimal as well.

Ruth was able to read her Bible, pray, sing, and welcome visitors. Ruth's pastor was involved from the beginning, and he visited once a week to counsel Ruth and to communicate with the hospice team. He counseled her in the areas of faith, hope, and love, focused on the promises of everlasting life to come, and reported changes he observed to the hospice nurse. The deacons set up a visitation schedule for members of the congregation to visit and provided for some of Ruth's material needs. Ruth was able to attend worship services on the Lord's Day, and the means of grace provided her with great strength and encouragement.

Her symptoms were controlled so well that she was able to sit through the entire service. She heard the preaching of the Word, she participated in a Lord's Supper, saw a baptism, sang praise to God, and enjoyed communion with the saints. She worshipped for a month and a half with the congregation before she could no longer attend services. A day after her last worship service, Ruth started to decline and was confined to her bed. Her body was weakening, and the medications lost their effectiveness. Ruth experienced increasing pain, short-ness of breath, and respiratory congestion. The hospice nurse managed these symptoms with various medications as well. As Ruth was nearing death, the pastor, elders, deacons, and many from the congregation came to visit. She lay peace-fully and sang in a low, slightly gurgled voice the refrain from the hymn "It is Well with My Soul." Eventually, with those she loved gathered around the room, she fell silent as she went into a coma, and a couple hours later she fell asleep in her Lord.

Concluding Comments

It has only been in the last seventy years that advances in medicine have boomed; but along with these great strides has come, for many Christians, an attitude of entitlement, dependency, and confusion. The pastor must be aware of this, and guard his flock against it. In a very real sense, Western medicine has become the only hope for people in our society, but it is not the Christian hope. The pastor has to know how to respond to the medical community and how to work within its context in order to lead his congregation biblically. He needs to be an expert, not in diagnosing, prescribing medications, or treating physical ailments, but in responding biblically to its underlying assumptions (Eph. 6:12). The pastor needs to know how to use medical science as the tool God intended it to be, and it is my prayer that *Pastoral Care and Western Medicine* will help him accomplish this goal.

Appendices

All of the following appendices are available in booklet form from Christian Community Care Press. To order copies, please visit: www.christiancommunitycarepress. com.

Appendix A

Pastor's Medical Care Handbook

Western Medicine Is NOT Neutral!

Christians Affirm the Following, Contrary to Western Medicine

- General (natural) and special (supernatural) revelation and that through special revelation, a philosophy about nature is developed.
- The universe is not a closed system; the LORD is sovereign over all, and the end will come when Jesus Christ returns.
- Life is purposeful and is determined by the mysterious providence of God.
- Nonliving objects are composed of material substance, but living creatures are composed of both material and immaterial substances.
- God is transcendent over and immanent in his creation.
- Human well-being is found in one's spiritual state with God, not in his physical state in the environment in which he lives.

Christians Reject the Following Concerning Western Medicine

- The assumption that our universe consists of one substance (materialism, physicalism, monism).
- The assumption that all is God and god is everything (pantheism).
- The belief that human beings can become self-actualized (humanism).
- The belief that we possess inner divinity and are therefore intrinsically good (New Age).
- The assumption that all religions are basically the same and it does not matter what you believe (deism, polytheism, and agnosticism).
- The assumption that mankind has evolved and is still evolving (atheism) and that through the exercise of our inbred god-consciousness (or self-actualization), we will bring about tranquility, harmony, and happiness.

Becoming a Part of the Healthcare Team

Pointers for Working with Healthcare Professionals

- Be humble, intelligent, and helpful.
- Don't have a critical spirit but be a critical thinker.
- Listen carefully to what healthcare team members have to say.
- Don't try to be the doctor or another member of the healthcare team—be the pastor.
- Know your limitations and the roles of other healthcare team members.

Integrating the Congregation into a Member's Hospice Care

- Notify the diaconal team (if your congregation has one) that the member has signed onto hospice.

- Pray publicly for the dying member and for the family in specific ways.
- The dying member and family should be discussed at each session and deacon meeting, and the following areas should be addressed:
  1. How are the dying member and the member's family doing spiritually and physically?
  2. What kinds of assistance is the church giving?
     A. At what level is the congregation involved?
     B. Is the assistance disseminated wisely?
     C. What further assistance is needed?
  3. What is the hospice team doing?
  4. How is the integration of the team working?

Body, Soul, Medications, and Biblical Counseling

Dangers in Misunderstanding the Body-and-Soul Relationship

- The soul is prior to the body in the sense that it gives the body life, consciousness, and intentionality, and without it the body is lifeless.
- Two extremes in the body-and-soul relationship must be avoided:
  1. Psychological experience emanates only from neurological function.
  2. Neurological experience emanates only from psychological processes.
- The soul must not be compartmentalized. The soul is one simple substance with different functions, and distinctions between the heart and the mind must be avoided when counseling. The greatest danger with a heart-mind dichotomy is the potential to fall into a form of behavioral psychology.

- Due to the intricate union of body and soul, physiological and anatomical changes may cause a person to sin.

Information to Gather when Counseling
- Discern to the best of your ability whether or not the person is a believer. If a person is not a Christian, then the goal of counseling must be evangelism.
- Gather accurate data:
  1. How was the condition diagnosed?
  2. What is the history of the condition?
  3. What effects has the condition had on the Christian's lifestyle?
  4. How does the condition impact the Christian's thinking and attitudes?
  5. How do relatives and friends respond to the Christian's condition?
  6. Is the Christian on any medications?

The Cornerstone of Biblical Counseling
- Maintain the homeostatic balance between the body and soul, which will require assessing:
  1. If medication is needed?
  2. If medication is *not* needed?

Caution: I understand that you are not a medical doctor, and it will be difficult to assess these matters. You cannot prescribe and should not withdraw medications, but you can refer the Christian, along with your *objective* assessment (i.e., client suffers from insomnia, hands are tremulous, cannot keep a conversation, alert but disorientated to person, place, and time, reports, "I will die if I stop taking my antianxiety medication," wringing of hands, lying about . . . , itching, etc.) and recommendations, to the healthcare professionals who can.

- Remember: you will not be able to counsel a person effectively if the homeostatic relationship between the body and soul is not achieved at some level.
- The reception of the Word of God through the means of grace.
- Constantly intertwine the triad of faith, hope, and love by applying the Word of God.
- Cultivate the Christian's relationship with the indwelling Spirit by encouraging self-denial, prayer, and meditation in accordance with the Word of God.

What to Address when Counseling (and Preaching)
- The Christian will need to understand how non-Christian health practitioners view illness, disease, and death.
- The Christian must be taught a biblical understanding of illness, disease, and death.
  1. The Christian needs to hear that the ultimate cause of affliction is sin, not blind, random processes.
  2. The Christian needs to know that his affliction is according to God's incomprehensible plan.
  3. The Christian needs to know that God is still in control, no matter how he feels.
- The Christian must be reminded that Jesus bore all of his afflictions, no matter how ill or diseased he may become.
- The Christian needs to understand that at present, God is using this affliction to sanctify him and to direct his eyes to Christ in deeper faith, hope, and love.
- The Christian must come to terms with the fact that this affliction is beneficial in some way. God is using it for his purposes, so it is up to him and not medical science to remove it.

- The Christian must be taught to promote good health as a steward, even if it means turning away from medical procedures that may cure the disease but destroy the body and disrupt the homeostatic relationship between the body and soul.
- You should seek to discern, to the best of your ability, when medical intervention is advantageous and when it is futile, and you should know how to counsel biblically in either case.
  1. If medical intervention is advantageous, then your counseling will be directed toward recovery.
  2. If medical intervention is futile, then your counseling will be directed toward comfort and accepting death.
- The goal of bodily stewardship, and not the healing of the body, must always be in the forefront of your thinking.
- It is important for you to understand the unified relationship of the body and the soul, which means addressing physical problems, inward thoughts, and outward actions.
- Your goal as a counselor is to facilitate an atmosphere in the body and soul that will be receptive to the Word of God, so that the Christian may receive it in faith, hope, and love by the power of the indwelling Spirit.
- Rooting out idolatry and encouraging dependence on God is the chief end of *all* biblical counseling.

Making Decisions Concerning Medical Care

Questions to Consider when Making Decisions about Medical Care

- How will this medical treatment help the Christian be a good steward of his or her body?

- How is this treatment going to assist the Christian in advancing the kingdom of God on earth?
- Will this treatment destroy the body and have the potential to fail in the end anyway?
- Does this treatment have the potential of making the Christian a long-term burden on others?

Important Truths to Remember when making Medical Decisions
- No matter how sick, diseased, or debilitated a Christian becomes, he is still in Christ and therefore is healed already.
- God in his providence uses illness, disease, and dying to sanctify Christians.
- The goal for the Christian is not healing but God's glory; for this reason, a great deal of biblical wisdom is required when making medical decisions in each individual case.

Pastoral Care and Counseling for End of Life
Medications and Hospice Care
- There are two major groups of medications that hospice agencies commonly use (see table A):
  1. Psychotropic drugs
  2. Narcotics
- Beware: these medications may have adverse and unwanted side effects, may be abused, and may cause an overdose.
- Beware: the medications may become an idol to the Christian, and it is usually a non-Christian healthcare professional, an idolater, who is administering them.
- It will be important for you to establish with the dying Christian the level of pain and discomfort he is willing to endure and, along with the dying member, to communicate this to the hospice clinician.

- The goal in using these medications is to maintain the homeostatic relationship between the body and soul in order to increase the Christian's devotion to God.
- Psychotropic drugs and narcotics can be used effectively to *maintain* mental stability and to provide important physical comfort to the Christian that will permit you to counsel effectively.
- You can assist the hospice team greatly by identifying physical and mental afflictions and reporting them so that the proper medications may be given and the dosages may be adjusted.
- You need to remember that as the dying Christian approaches death, significant changes will occur not only physically but also mentally, and extremely high dosages and several different types of medications may be required to effectively to treat the signs and symptoms that develop (see table B).
- When a Christian is actively dying, the pain and suffering may become so unbearable that total sedation may be required (Prov. 31:6).

End-of-Life Counseling
- Where counseling should begin on end-of-life issues depends on how well the dying person and the person's family are coping with the impending death.
- No matter where you begin, four hopeful teachings should be consciously and continuously intertwined:
    1. Remind the dying Christian of the victory that Christ has over death (1 Cor. 15:55).
    2. Communicate the assurance that Jesus will never leave or forsake the Christian (John 10:27–29; Rom. 8:31–39).

3. Address the Christian's many questions in light of Scripture. Give honest answers in light of the Scriptures, even if they are hard to receive (use wisdom and tact in presenting those answers of course).
4. Remind the Christian of the promises of eternal life (Rev. 21:1–4; 22:1–5).

- Plan the funeral with the dying Christian and family.
- At all times remember to pray and sing psalms, hymns, and spiritual songs with the dying Christian and his family.
- After the death, provide bereavement counseling for the family. A recommended visitation schedule is as follows: visit the closest family members daily for a few days until the funeral, then weekly for four weeks, monthly for the next two months, and periodically thereafter.
- Counseling should initially focus on helping the family members grieve. Next, help the family process the death biblically, and, finally, encourage them to move on in fervent service for Christ.
- Remember that the impact of the death does not usually hit the family until a month or two later.

Table A: **Commonly Used Psychotropic Drugs and Narcotics**

Psychotropic Drugs
Medications: lorazepam; diazepam
Uses: Anxiety, restlessness, difficulty sleeping
Side Effects: drowsiness, forgetfulness, dizziness, weakness, confusion
Adverse Reactions (particular in the elderly): risk of falling, severe agitation or confusion, hallucinations, agitation, confusion

Medications: haloperidol; olanzepine; chlorpromazine
Uses: Hallucinations, agitation, confusion, mania
Side Effects: drowsiness, dry mouth, slow breathing
Adverse Reactions: risk of falling, severe agitation or
confusion

Medications: prochlorperazine; metoclopramide;
chlorpromazine
Uses: Nausea and vomiting
Side Effects: dizziness, sleepiness, restlessness, tremor,
dry mouth, constipation or diarrhea
Adverse Reaction: increased nausea

Medications: Phenobarbital; diazepam
Uses: Seizures
Side Effects: drowsiness, hallucinations, flushing,
nausea, "hangover headache"
Adverse Reactions: risk of falling, severe agitation

Medications: diphenhydramine; lorazepam; temazepam
Uses: Insomnia
Side Effects: drowsiness, dizziness
Adverse Reactions: risk of falling, severe irritability or
anxiety

*It is also important to note that antidepressant medica-
tions are sometimes used to control neurological pain (sharp,
tingling, or burning pain). If the hospice clinician desires to
use an antidepressant, it is not necessarily for depression,
although it may be. It will be important to find out if the antidepressant is used for depression. Some of the most common
antidepressants used in hospice are: neurontin, nortriptyline,
trazadone, venlafaxine, amitriptyline, paroxetine, fluoxetine,
mirtazapine, bupropion and sertraline.*

Narcotics

Medications: morphine; oxycodone; hydromorphone; fentanyl
Uses: Pain management
Side Effects: drowsiness, dizziness, confusion, constipation, hallucinations, nausea, difficulty urinating, rash, itch; risk of withdrawal symptoms if stopped abruptly (nausea, cramps)
Adverse Reactions: risk of falling, constipation; very slow breathing.

Table B: Signs and Symptoms that May Occur as a Person Nears Death

Months to Two Weeks
1. Isolation and withdrawal
2. Poor appetite
3. Increased sleep
4. Less communication

Two Weeks to One Week
1. Confusion
2. Restlessness
3. Talking to unseen people (hallucinations and delusions).
4. Pulling off blankets and clothing
5. Physical signs and symptoms
   A. Color changes to the skin
   B. Increased sweating
   C. Irregular breathing
   D. Congestion and raspy breathing
   E. Sleeping but responding to touch
   F. Complaints of the body feeling heavy and fatigued

   G. Insignificant food and fluid intake
   H. Body temperature may be either hot or cold

Six Days to One Hour
1. Sudden surge of energy
2. Intensification of one-to-two-week signs and symptoms
   A. Glassy eyes, cloudy, tearing, fixated, and half open eyes
   B. Irregular breathing patterns with long pauses between breaths
   C. Increased restlessness or no movement at all
   D. Purplish feet and hands

Minutes
1. Gasping for air like a fish out of water
2. Totally unable to be aroused
3. Cold, clammy, pale, gray, ashen, or bluish body

Appendix B

Medicine for the Body and Soul: "Songs in the Night"

Charles Haddon Spurgeon (1834-1892), the prince of preachers, was a Calvinist Baptist minister. He preached for thirty-eight years at the Metropolitan Tabernacle in London, England, under constant illness, physical pain, and depression. By the age of thirty-five, he had experienced his first attack of painful gout, was diagnosed with rheumatism, and suffered from a condition called Bright's disease (inflammation of the kidneys). Prior to these physical problems, Spurgeon suffered from depression, which started at the age of twenty-four, just two years after he entered the ministry. Depression, and his other illnesses, would be Spurgeon's lifelong companions until he entered his everlasting rest in 1892.

Sometime during the mid- to late1800s, Spurgeon preached a sermon called "Songs in the Night."[1] This sermon is a masterpiece of counsel to those under affliction. It is a sermon forged in the body and soul of an experienced

---

[1] Charles Spurgeon, *Sermons* (Grand Rapids: Baker, 1996), 2:167-87.

sufferer, gifted preacher, and doctor of souls. He opens the sermon with these introductory comments:

> Surely, if men be tried and troubled exceedingly, it is because, while they think about their troubles and distress themselves about their fears, they do not say, "Where is God my Maker, who gives songs in the night?" . . . The greatest cause of the Christian's distress, the reason of the depths of sorrow into which many believers are plunged, is simply this— that while they are looking about, on the right hand and on the left, to seek how they may escape their troubles, they forget to look to the hills whence all real help comes; they do not say, "Where is God my Maker, who gives songs in the night?"

The biggest problem for Christians when they experience illness or disease or face death is that they seek to escape it, says Spurgeon, rather than look to God for help in the midst of it. "Night is the season of terror and alarm to most men . . . nights of sorrow, nights of persecution, nights of doubt, nights of bewilderment, nights of anxiety, nights of oppression, nights of ignorance—nights of all kinds, which press upon our spirits and terrify our souls." "But," he goes on, "blessed be God, the Christian . . . can say, 'My God gives me songs in the night.'"

After his introduction Spurgeon breaks his sermon into four points. First is the source of songs in the night, which is God. Second is the content for songs in the night. Third is the excellence of songs in the night. Fourth is the uses and benefits of songs in the night to ourselves and others.

The Source for Songs in the Night—God
Spurgeon writes,

> Any fool can [sing] in the day. When the cup is full, man draws inspiration from it; when wealth rolls in abundance around him, any man can sing to the praise of God. . . . Let this voice be free, and this body full of health, and I can sing God's praise; but stop this tongue, lay upon me the bed of languishing, and it is not so easy to sing from the bed, and chant high praises in the fires. Give me the bliss of spiritual liberty, and let me mount up to my God, get near the throne, and I will sing, ay, sing as sweet as seraphs; but confine me, fetter my spirit, clip my wings, make me exceeding sad, so that I become old like the eagle—ah! Then it is hard to sing. It is not in man's power to sing, when all is adverse. . . . Songs in the night come only from God; they are not in the power of man.

God is the author of songs in the night. "It is strange," writes Spurgeon, "when God gives his children mercies, they generally set their hearts more on the mercies than on the Giver of them; but when night comes, and he sweeps all the mercies away, then at once they say, 'Now, my God, I have nothing to sing of but you; I must come to you; and to you only. . . . It is in the night we sing of God, and of God alone."

God is the one who inspires songs in the night, says Spurgeon. All human comforters will fail, but in the night, God succeeds. Comfort "him as you may," says Spurgeon, "it will be only a woeful note or two of mournful resignation that you will get from him; you will get no psalms of praise, no hallelujahs, no sonnets."

But let God come to his child in the night, let him whisper in his ear as he lies on his bed, and how you see his eyes flash fire in the night! Do you not hear him say, "Tis, paradise, if Thou art here; If Thou depart, tis hell." . . . It is marvelous, brethren, how one sweet word of God will make whole songs for Christians. One word of God is like a piece of gold, and the Christian is the gold-beater, and he can hammer that promise out for whole weeks. . . . The Christian gets his songs from God: God gives him inspiration, and teaches him how to sing: "God my Maker, who gives songs in the night."

Spurgeon instructs the afflicted believer, "Do not go to this comforter or that . . . but go first and foremost to your Maker, for he is the great composer of songs and teacher of music; he it is who can teach you to sing."

The Content for Songs in the Night

There are three things the Christian should sing about, says Spurgeon. First, sing about things yesterday. Second, sing about the night itself. Third, sing about tomorrow.

"Christian," Spurgeon says, "perhaps the best song you can sing, to cheer you in the night, is the song of yester-morn. . . . remember that God, who made you sing yesterday, has not left you in the night . . . though he has left you a little, it is to prove you, to make you trust him better, and serve him more." Sing of God's "electing love and covenanted mercies . . . that blessed decree wherein you were ordained to eternal life . . . that glorious Man who undertook your redemption . . . that solemn covenant signed, and sealed, and ratified, in all things ordered well." If you cannot sing of this, then sing of the mercies you experienced in the past. "What!" says Spurgeon, "Man, cannot you . . . sing of a little of that blessed hour when Jesus met you?" For "you are able to sing: 'I am forgiven, I am forgiven' 'A monument of grace, a sinner saved by blood.'"

Come, man! I beseech you, go to the river of your experience, and pull up a few bulrushes, and weave them into an ark, wherein your infant faith may float safely on the stream. I bid you do not forget what God has done. . . . go back, then, a little way, and take the mercies of yesterday; and though it is dark now, light the lamps of yesterday, and they shall glitter through the darkness, and you shall find that God has given you a song in the night.

"Ay," says one, "but you know, that when we are in the dark, we cannot see the mercies God has given us. . . . I know they are good strong promises, but I cannot get near enough . . . that is the difficulty." . . . If God has never been kind to you, one thing you surely know, and that is, he has been kind to others. . . . O Christian! Only think of what he has done for others. . . . Thus, Christian, you will get a song in the night out of other people, if you cannot get a song from yourself. Never be ashamed of taking a leaf out of another man's experience book.

Perhaps you cannot find a song from yesterday, says Spurgeon. Then look to the night itself, he says,

For there is one thing I am sure we can sing about, let the night be ever so dark, and that is, "It is of the Lord's mercies that we are not consumed, and because his compassion fails not." If we cannot sing very loud, yet we can sing a little low tune, something like this—"He hath not dealt with us after our sins, nor rewarded us according to our iniquities." .

. . Christian, you will always have one thing to sing about—"Lord, I thank you, it is not all darkness!" . . . However dark it may be, I think you may find some little comfort, some little joy, some little mercy left, and some little promise to cheer your spirit. . . . If you have only one [mercy], bless God for that one, perhaps he will make it two; and if you have only two [mercies], bless God twice for the two [mercies], and perhaps he will make them four. Try, then, if you cannot find a song in the night.

Or maybe the night is just too dark, and yesterday is a distant dream. Then, Spurgeon says, sing of the day that is to come.

Often do I cheer myself with the thought of the coming of the Lord. . . . For that day do I look; it is to the bright horizon of that second coming that I turn my eyes . . . cheer up your heart with the thought of the coming of your Lord. Be patient, for "Lo! He comes, with clouds descending." Be patient! The husbandman waits until he reaps his harvest. Be patient; for you know who has said, "Behold, I come quickly, and my reward is with me, to give to every man according as his works shall be."

One thought more upon that point. There is another sweet tomorrow of which we hope to sing in the night. Soon, beloved, you and I shall lie on our dying bed, and we shall want a song in the night then; and I do not know where we shall get it, if we do not get it from the tomorrow. Kneeling by the bed of an apparently dying saint, last night, I said, "Well, sister, he has been precious to you; you can rejoice in his covenant mercies, and his past loving-kindnesses." She put out her hand, and said, "Ah! Sir, do not talk about them now; I want the sinner's Savior as much now as ever; it is not a saint's Savior I want; it is still a sinner's Savior that I am in need of, for I am a sinner still." I found that I could not comfort her with the past; so I reminded her of the golden streets, of the gates of pearl, of the walls of jasper, of the harps of gold, of the songs of bliss; and then her eye glistened; she said, "Yes, I shall be there soon; I shall meet them by-and-by;" and then she seemed so glad! Ah! I believe, you may always cheer yourself with that thought; for if you are ever so low now, remember that "A few more rolling suns, at most, Will land thee on fair Canaan's coast."

The Excellence of Songs in the Night

"It is the easiest thing in the world to open your mouth, and let the words come out; but when the devil puts his hand over your mouth, can you sing then?" If you can, then that "is hearty singing; that is a real song that springs from the heart." Not only will songs in the night be hearty, but they will also be lasting.

It will not do to sing one of those light songs when death and you are having the last tug. It will not do to enter heaven singing one of those unchaste, unholy sonnets. No; but the Christian who can sing in the night will not have to leave off his song; he may keep on singing it forever. He may put his foot on Jordan's stream, and continue his melody; he may wade through it, and keep on singing still, and land himself safe in heaven; and when he is there, there need not be a gap in his strain, but in a nobler, sweeter strain, he may still continue singing his power to save.

Songs in the night demonstrate real faith, true courage, and true love, says Spurgeon.

> To believe in Christ when he is shrouded in darkness, to stick hard and fast by the Savior when all men speak ill of him and forsake him—that is true faith. He who sings a song to Christ in the night, sings the best song in all the world; for he sings from the heart.

The Uses and Benefits of Songs in the Night for Ourselves and Others

It is very useful to sing in the night because it will cheer the soul. "Keep your mouth full of songs," says Spurgeon, "and you will often keep your heart full of praises; keep on singing as long as you can [and] you will find it a good method of driving away your fears." Spurgeon goes on to say that God loves to hear his children singing in the night, for it pleases him. Songs in the night will cheer our companions as well, says Spurgeon, and they will preach the gospel to our non-Christian neighbors.

> O, Christian, instead of disputing, let me tell you how to prove your religion. Live it out! Live it out! Give the external as well as the internal evidence; give the external evidence of your own life. You are sick; there is your neighbor, who laughs at religion; let him come into your house. When he was sick, he said, "O, send for the doctor;" and there he was fretting, and fuming, and whining, and making all manner of noises. When you are sick, send for him; tell him that you are resigned to the Lord's will; that you will kiss the chastening rod; that you will take the cup, and drink it, because your Father gives it. You need not make a boast of this, or it will lose all

its power; but do it because you cannot help doing it. Your neighbor will say, "There is something in that." And when you come to the borders of the grave—he was there once, and you heard how he shrieked, and how frightened he was—give him your hand, and say to him, "Ah! I have a Christ that will do to die by; I have a religion that will make me sing in the night." Let him hear how you can sing, "Victory, victory, victory!" Through him that loved you. I tell you, we may preach fifty thousand sermons to prove the gospel, but we shall not prove it half so well as you will through singing in the night. Keep a cheerful frame; keep a happy heart; keep a contented spirit; keep your eye up, and your heart aloft, and you will prove Christianity.

There is a dreadful night coming for some "where there will be no songs of joy," says Spurgeon.

There is a night coming when a song shall be sung, of which misery shall be the subject, set to the music of wailing and gnashing of teeth; there is a night coming when woe, unutterable woe, shall be the matter of an awful terrific *Miserere*—when the orchestra shall be composed of damned men, and howling fiends, and yelling demons; and mark you, I speak what I do know, and testify the Scriptures. There is a night coming for a poor soul . . . and unless he repent it will be a night wherein he will have to growl, and howl, and sigh, and cry, and moan and groan forever.

Appendix C

Thomas Halyburton: A Story of Reality and Hope

Thomas Halyburton (1674-1712), a Scottish theologian and pastor, provides insight into the physical and spiritual struggles that a Christian may experience as death nears. In his memoirs the last six days of his life on earth are vividly recorded by his friends.[1] At the age of thirty-seven, "a dangerous sickness seized," Halyburton, "which obliged the physicians at several times to take from him about forty-four ounces of blood." He recovered briefly (surely not from the bloodletting), but a year later the young Halyburton became ill again. His arms and legs swelled, and he became weak and debilitated. He probably suffered from a condition called lymphedema, which was either hereditary or caused by cancer, most likely the latter.[2] On September 17, 1712,

---

[1] Thomas Halyburton, *Memoirs of Thomas Halyburton*, ed. Joel R. Beeke (Grand Rapids: Reformation Heritage Books, 1996), 226–94.

[2] Lymphedema occurs when a person's lymph vessels, which are similar to veins, are unable to adequately drain fluid that carries waste products from the arm or leg. The lymphatic system is crucial in keeping the body healthy. It circulates protein-rich lymph fluid throughout the

Halyburton became totally bedridden, and on the twenty-third day of September, "he fell asleep in the Lord."

Wednesday, September 17

The scene in Halyburton's home, even in the midst of death, was warm and pleasant. His family was constantly present, and several visitors came and went. A family physician stopped in from time to time to assess Halyburton's status, and a pharmacist was on hand to provide medication for the management of his symptoms. Several ministers, from far and near visited, and several members from his congregation stopped by. Even his servants took time to visit! Halyburton was loved by many people, and even while he was dying, his love for them was expressed just as deeply.

Halyburton struggled with fear of death, depression, and desertion by God. When he was asked how he rested the night of September 16, he said, "Not well." He reported that he was struggling with assurance of faith in God, for he felt God's condemnation weighing heavy upon him, "and all that is difficult in death to a saint." He went on to say, "All my enemies have been roundabout me," spiritual enemies such as doubt and despondency and weak faith. Halyburton's desire, however, was to be kept "in this last trial" so that he would not be an "offense to His people." Halyburton was concerned that his struggle with assurance, depression, desertion, doubt, and despondency would cause others to question their faith in God and stumble.

---

body, collecting bacteria, viruses, and waste products. The lymphatic system then carries these through lymph vessels, which lead to lymph nodes. The wastes are filtered out of the body by lymphocytes (infection-fighting cells that live in your lymph nodes). In certain conditions, such as cancer or rare hereditary diseases, the lymph nodes and vessels can become occluded, and swelling (edema) will occur.

Thursday, September 18

Oh, what a terrible conflict I had yesterday! But now I can say, "I have fought the good fight, I have kept the faith." Now He had filled my mouth with a new song, Jehovah-jireh—in the mount of the Lord. Praise, praise, is comely for the upright. Shortly I shall get another sight of God than ever I had, and be more [able] to praise Him. . . . Oh the thoughts of an incarnate God are sweet and ravishing! And oh how [I] wonder at myself, that I do not love Him more—that I do not admire Him more! Oh that I could honor Him! What a wonder that I enjoy such composure under all my bodily trouble, and in view of approaching death! [Then turning to his wife he said] He came to me in the third watch of the night, walking upon the waters; and He said to me, "I am Alpha and Omega, the beginning and the end; I was dead and am alive." . . . He stilled the tempest, and oh there is a sweet calm in my soul!

Halyburton was delivered from the conflict he experienced the day before. As a result he was filled with words of praise, and his thoughts were focused upon Jesus. Halyburton had an experience that was defined by Scripture. He considered Jesus walking on the water (Matt. 14:22-33), stilling the storm (Mark 4:35-41), and the words from Revelation 22:13. The Holy Spirit applied these words to his soul, and the result was peace and comfort. This experience was so powerful that this experienced Doctor of Divinity said, "The little acquaintance I have had with God within these two days has been better than ten thousand times the pains I have all my life been about religion."

Halyburton's thinking was reoriented through the experience, and now he sought fervently to commend everyone around him to Christ, particularly those in his family.

I preached the gospel of Christ with pleasure, and I loved it; for my own soul's salvation was upon it; and since I lay down, I have not changed thoughts about it. I commend it to you all, to make it your business to double your diligence. There may be hard conflicts. You have a prospect of difficulties between you and the grave. We are all quite untried; but we . . . need to have on the whole armor of God—to watch and be sober.

Seek the Lord, and be real in religion; content not yourself with the form of it; a mere profession will not do the turn. This will be but the shell without the kernel; but they that are sincere shall inherit the crown. Let not the scorn and contempt cast on religion cause you to give it up. It is not in vain to seek the Lord; you have found it. The Scriptures of truth are a contemned [reviled] book by men; but they are "able to make you wise unto salvation."

The struggle was not over yet, however.

Later that evening Halyburton experienced some physical changes, and the inner conflict started again. He said, "I know not how it comes to pass that a body that has met with so much of God should be so unthankful, as in the least to doubt him about the rest," and lamented "What an evil heart of unbelief, cursed unbelief and cursed self, have I!" This time a friend ministered to him by reading 1 Thessalonians 1:4 and chapter 5, and 2 Corinthians 1:1-11. Halyburton commented, after the reading, and prior to his retiring for the night,

Now there it all is. God has delivered and filled me with peace, when I was under that heavy depression. I hope that He will deliver, even from that which I feared in death, and let me find that I have got the victory, and that "the God of peace will bruise Satan shortly under my feet," and he will get up no more; and I will get victory over the cunning world—the deceitful heart. Oh many a weary day I have had with my unbelief! If I had faith to believe things not seen—if I had faith answerable to the convictions I had on my soul, that my happiness lay not in the things seen and temporal, but eternal—if I had had faith's abiding impressions realizing these things, I would not have known how to abide out of heaven a moment.

Friday, September 19

After a restless night, Halyburton awoke at five in the morning. He was instructed to lie quietly and continue to get some rest, but instead he replied, "No, no; should I lie here altogether useless? Should not I spend the last bit of my strength to show forth His glory?" Then "he held up his hands, and said: 'Lame hands and lame legs; but see a lame man leaping and rejoicing.'" Soon after, his family awoke and gathered around his bedside, and he spoke to them about his impending death. Later that morning some visitors came by, and with a group of people congregated around his bed, he spoke these words:

Here is a demonstration of the reality of religion, that I, a poor weak, timorous man, as much once afraid of death as any—I that have been many years under the terrors of death—come now, in the mercy of God, and by the power of His grace, composedly, and with joy, to look death in the face. I have seen it in its paleness, and all the circumstances of horror attending it; I dare look it in the face in its most ghastly shape, and hope in a little while to have the victory. . . . I hope he will deal tenderly. But pray for me, that my faith fail not; I loved to live preaching Christ, and love to die preaching Christ.

Thereafter he said . . . what shall we say of the Lord Christ? He is altogether lovely. Religion is a mystery; but I was looking through the promises this night, and observing how to provide against the last conflict; I was astonished, and at a stand, when I saw the sweet accomplishment of them. Every promise of the Word of God is sweet; they are sure promises. Oh, sirs, study the Word; observe the accomplishment of it. It was the thing I loved all my days, and it is sweet to the last. Oh, the accomplishment of the Word is worthy to be observed, and especially when I was looking this same night to what He has already fulfilled for me.

Then the exhausted, weak, and suffering, Halyburton turned to his wife and children and with deepest sympathy he sought closure with them and commended them to the ministers present.

I recommend [my wife] to your care. She has been a friend of my bosom, the wife of my youth—a faithful friend. . . . Oh sirs, check my poor babies if you see anything in them disorderly. . . . "Patience must have its perfect work;" I will wait for it. "My soul longs more than that watch for the morning." Sweet Lord Jesus, make haste, until the day break, and the shadows flee away. . . . pray a word for patience for me to bide this last trial.

Later that evening the physician visited, and the declining Halyburton said: I have been studying the promises [for fifteen years]; but I have seen more of the book of God this night than [my fifteen years of study]. Oh, the wisdom that is laid up in the Book

of God, that is to be found only there! . . . I know a
. . . dying man will [usually become delirious]; but
I bless God He has so kept the little judgment I had,
that I have been capable to reflect with composure
on His dealing with me. I am sober and composed,
if ever I was sober; and whether men will forbear, or
whether they will hear, this is a testimony. The operations of the Spirit of God are maligned this day; but
if we take away the operations and influences of the
Spirit of God in religion, I know not what is left. He
promised the Spirit to lead us into all truth. . . . There
is a sweet composure on my spirit; the beams of the
house [body] are, as it were, cracking. I am laying
down my tabernacle [body], to be built again. Oh to
get grace to be faithful to death! For after we have
gone through many things, yet we have need still to
wait on God till the last; for it is he that endures to
the end that shall be saved. Am not I a man wonderfully upheld by God under affliction and death? . . . I
fancy my feet are growing cold, doctor; yea, yea, all
the parts of this body are going to ruin.

After speaking to the physician, he dictated a letter to his
nephew and retired for the night. In the letter he said:

I have found a full proof that religion is a real, useful,
noble, and profitable thing. I have been helped,
through the mercy of God, during my lying here, to
rejoice in the goodness of God, and lie composedly
and pleasantly. Nothing but religion, nothing but the
power of the grace of God, can have that efficacy to
enable me to do so; and having found it so reliable
a friend, I could not but commend it to you. . . . but
it must be a renewing work of grace that will fix an
abiding anchor. The Lord in mercy engage your heart

to Him, that you may find how good He is to the soul that seeks Him, as I do this day to my joy, and hope to do more fully in a little. I could not but commend the Lord to you, having found so much of His goodness. I never found so much when I was in health and prosperity, as I find now in sickness and languishing. I find He makes all things to be His people's for good; sickness, or health, or diseases, or whatever they be, all is good; and I find all for good.

Saturday, September 20

As visitors arrived Halyburton was drinking "a little wine for refreshment," and his countenance was lifted briefly. To those around him he said:

Oh, this is the most honorable pulpit that ever I was in! I am preaching the same Christ, the same holiness, the same happiness I did before. I have much satisfaction in that. I am not ashamed of it all my days, and I am not ashamed of it at the last, when I am put to the trial of the bed of languishing. Blessed be God, we are all agreed in that, that it is the power of God to salvation.

Soon the refreshment wore off, however, and pain, suffering, and affliction visited Halyburton with a vengeance.

Here I die, saying, "Lord Jesus, receive my spirit." Come, sweet Lord Jesus, receive this spirit, fluttering within my breast like a bird to be out of a snare. When shall I hear Him say, "Arise, my love, my fair one, and come away; the winter is past, the rain is over and gone?" Come, sweet Lord Jesus, come and take me by the hand, [so] that I stumble not in the dark valley of death.

Seeing his wife weeping, Halyburton said to her,

> Oh my sweet bird, are you there? I am no more
> [yours]; I am the Lord's. I remember on the day I
> took you by the hand, I thought on parting with you,
> but I did not know how to get my heart off you again;
> but now I have got it done. Will . . . you give me
> to the Lord, my dear? . . . My dear, do not weep;
> you should rather rejoice. Rejoice with me, and let
> us exalt His Name together. I shall be in the same
> family with you; you must . . . stay a while behind,
> and take care of God's [children].

Finally, to all who were gathered around his bed, the dying
Halyburton said,

> You can see affliction is no mark of God's displea-
> sure. I often wondered how the martyrs could clap
> their hands in the fire; I do not wonder at it now. I
> could clap my hands, though you should hold burning
> candles about them, and think it no hardship though
> the flames were going round about them. And yet I
> would cry, and not be able to bear it . . . if the Lord
> withdrew.

Sunday, September 21

At three in the morning, Halyburton awoke and asked,
"Is it the Sabbath?" Halyburton had declined signifi-
cantly throughout the course of the day and into the night
on Saturday. On Sunday morning he was in great physical
distress with increased pain, fever, breathlessness, respiratory congestion, nausea, vomiting, and bouts of coughing.
Also the enemies of doubt, depression, and despondency
were afflicting his soul as well. In an afflicted voice he said,

> Even while under God and His goodness, I have been
> kept under a continual fear of my ill heart. These are
> the two worst enemies I have—self, with its fair
> shows and secret insinuations; and unbelief, strug-
> gling hard against me.

As the time for corporate worship approached, his family
departed, and one of the ministers stayed behind and cared
for Halyburton. Soon after the service, many came to see
Halyburton, gathered around his bed, and sang praise to God,
and the preacher gave a word of exhortation. The lethargic
Halyburton was pleased, and he rejoiced greatly.

Monday, September 22
Monday was a day that began with painful suffering as
well.

> God is melting me down into corruption and dust,
> and yet He is keeping me . . . calm. Oh, "who is
> like unto our God?" "Not unto us, not unto us, but
> to Thy Name, oh Lord, be the praise." "Our light
> afflictions, that endure but for a moment, work out
> for us a far more exceeding and eternal weight of
> glory." I shall get the martyr's crown, with a minister
> of Christ's crown; and oh, the martyr's crown is a
> glorious crown! I am now a witness for Christ, for
> the reality of religion; and I am suffering. It is given
> unto me not only to believe, but to suffer for His
> Name. I sought an increase of faith from our Lord
> Jesus, and our Lord has heard me; and now it is but
> a little, and I shall get the crown. And though there
> be a little [noisiness (secretions in his throat, called a
> death rattle)] about me, yet I am willing that you be
> spectators of it; for it is not for my sake that I meet

with this, but for your establishment. Is there not a beauty in this providence?

Then, suddenly, a burst of energy broke in on Halyburton, and he commented on the warmth of his body and the clarity of his mind.

> Strange! said he, this body is wasting away to corruption; and yet my intellect is so lively, that I cannot say there is the least alteration, the least decay of judgment or memory; such vigorous [acts] of my spirit toward God, and things that are not seen! But, said he, not I, not I, but the grace of God in me. "Not unto us, not unto us," which [I] still must have on my heart, since cursed self is apt to steal glory from God: here I must watch lest the enemy give me a wound.

The burst left just as quickly as it came and later that night Halyburton entered a semi-comatose state. During this time he went in and out of consciousness, and in a low gurgling speech he spoke of the end. In great pain, suffering, agony, breathlessness, nausea, vomiting, and choking, he began to cry out, "Lord, pity! . . . Pity, pity, Lord!"

One of the people present said, "You have been crying much to God, that He would be with you; and I doubt not but you are finding it now." Then another replied, "Yes . . . Now you are putting your seal to that truth . . . 'great is the gain of godliness.'" Somebody else agreed to what was said and went on to say, "I hope you are encouraging yourself in the Lord." Then Halyburton raised his exhausted arms and started to clap his hands. For the next six hours Halyburton was, for the most part, unresponsive. Prayer was offered on his behalf until he entered his everlasting rest with his Lord about seven in the morning on September 23, 1712.

Appendix D

The Christian and Advance Directives

An advance directive describes the type of medical care a person would like to have in the event that he cannot speak for himself due to an illness, disease, or traumatic injury. Laws for advance directives vary from state to state,[1] but the three main documents are: a living will, durable healthcare power of attorney, and a do-not-resuscitate order (DNR).

A living will is a written, legal document that describes specifically the kind of medical or life-sustaining treatments desired if a person becomes seriously or terminally ill. It defines a person's wishes, and it will assist others in making medical decisions when the person cannot speak for himself. Most living wills devote sections to list healthcare surrogates (proxies) and a person's desires concerning organ donations. A second advance directive is a durable healthcare power of attorney. A durable healthcare power of attorney is a legal document that identifies a person(s) chosen to make

---

[1] See this Web site for your state's advance directives: www.caringinfo. org/stateaddownload.

medical decisions on behalf of another person. The document becomes active any time a person is unconscious or unable to make medical decisions. It is important to make sure that the healthcare surrogate(s) on the living will is the same as the one(s) listed on the durable healthcare power of attorney. A third advance directive is a "do-not-resuscitate" order (DNR), which must be prepared by a physician at a person's request. A DNR is a written document that states that a person does not want cardiopulmonary resuscitation (CPR) if his heart stops beating or if he stops breathing. Any person who is eighteen years of age or older is able to prepare advance directives.

Advance directives are an effective way to make decisions concerning medical care in the event a person is not able to do so himself; this is very important for Christians. The documents are easy to prepare, but they require the signature of two witnesses, and in some states they may need to be notarized. Advance directives may be changed and rewritten at any time, provided the person is of a sound mind. If advance directives are changed or rewritten, a person must be sure to destroy any prior copies of them in order to eliminate confusion. It is also important for the primary physician and each of the healthcare surrogates to possess copies of all the documents.

Challenges in Advance Directives for Christians

The Christian will encounter challenges in drafting and implementing advance directives due to the ongoing progress in medical science. Medical science has provided many welcomed advances, but it also has created profound moral and ethical dilemmas with advancing technology and treatments. Less than seventy years ago, the options for treatment of the critically ill were limited and, consequently, so were medical options. Now, with advances in medical and technological treatments, such as cardiopulmonary resuscitation (CPR), defibrillation, mechanical ventilation, kidney dialysis, organ transplants, surgical procedures, antibiotics, cancer chemotherapy and radiation treatments, intravenous infusions, feeding tubes, a seriously ill person who probably would have died years earlier can be kept alive. Thus, the need for biblically informed advance directives is important.

The way the medical community defines life and death also poses significant challenges for the Christian. Before the middle of the twentieth century, death was defined simply as the absence of cardiac and respiratory function—a definition that is thoroughly biblical.[2] In the 1960s, however, it became increasingly possible to reverse cardiac and respiratory arrest through the use of CPR, defibrillation, mechanical ventilation, medications, and other treatments. Now, cardiac arrest and respiratory failure do not define death but rather a state called "clinical death." Technological advances have enabled the medical community to reverse the state of clinical death, though often it is at the expense of brain function. As a response to the ability to resuscitate individuals and keep them alive mechanically, "brain death" has now emerged as the legal definition of death.

In 1981, a presidential commission issued a landmark report called *Defining Death: Medical, Legal, and Ethical Issues in the Determination of Death.* This report is the basis for the "Uniform Definition of Death Act," which is now law in almost all fifty states. Using brain-death criteria, a physician can declare a person legally dead, even if the body is alive but does not have "brain function." The Act reads:

An individual who has sustained either (1) irreversible cessation of circulatory and respiratory functions, or (2) irreversible cessation of all functions of

---

[2] Josh. 11:11ff.; 1 Kings 15:29; 17:17; Job 27:3; Ps. 104:29; Isa. 2:22; cf. Gen. 2:7; 6:17; 7:15, 22; Ezek. 37:5ff.; Acts 17:25

the entire brain, including the brain stem, is dead. A determination of death must be made in accordance with accepted medical standards.[3]

There are major difficulties with this Act for the Christian. What does "irreversible" mean, and who or what decides what is irreversible? Irreversibility is based upon "accepted medical standards," which usually means human functionality as indicated by mechanical instrumentation (EEG, CT scan, or MRI) and a physician's subjective assessment. Christians value life, even if that life is functionally deficient and is "brain dead." Any definition of death based upon brain-death criteria is unacceptable for Christians.

Biblically, a person is dead when the heart and lungs have ceased to function. If there is no breathing and no heartbeat, there will be no brain function, and it is at this time that a person may be pronounced dead. This means that if a person is on artificial life support and has been diagnosed as being "brain dead," it will be necessary to withdraw the life support apparatus to see if he is truly dead. If the apparatus is removed, however, and the heart and lungs function, then the person is not dead, even if the so-called "brain dead" condition persists, and even if it is said to be "irreversible" by diagnostic equipment and a team of expert medical doctor(s).

Drafting Advance Directives

It is important to fill out advance directives as specifically as possible to ensure that biblically oriented care will be carried out. Living wills, if not explained with specific parameters, may empower physicians to determine when life-sustaining treatments are futile and allow them to with-

---

[3] The full report can be found at: https://idea.iupui. edu/dspace/handle/1805/707.

hold or withdraw treatment at their own discretion. In light of what was written above, this is something Christians do not desire. It is also important for Christians to eliminate undue stress on others by communicating their exact wishes concerning their medical care if they become incapacitated. Completing advance directives will enable Christians to state their wishes concerning medical care in a biblically oriented way.

When writing advance directives, it is important for Christians to make their desires clear in the following areas: CPR, mechanical ventilation, feeding tubes, intravenous infusions, blood products, surgeries, invasive diagnostic tests, kidney dialysis, and antibiotics. A living will indicates a person's desires concerning these invasive procedures when he cannot speak for himself.

In constructing a biblically oriented living will, it will be necessary to consider the following. First, if a person is connected to life support, it is never wrong for Christians to remove it. I grant that a lot of factors are involved and great medical and biblical wisdom must be exercised in such cases, but it is God who determines when a person lives or dies and not the life-support apparatus (Eccles. 3:2). In fact, in most cases, it will be necessary to remove the life support in order to see if a "brain dead" person is truly dead. Cessation of heart and lung function determines death biblically, not unresponsiveness. Second, if a person is removed from life support and the heart and lungs function independently of the equipment, a precedent has been established to sustain that person's life (Job 1:21; 33:4). This leads to the third matter: sustaining life does not necessarily mean aggressive medical treatment in the future, such as CPR, defibrillation, mechanical ventilation, intravenous infusions, blood products, surgeries, invasive diagnostic tests, kidney dialysis, and antibiotics, but it does mean nutritional sustenance and hydration (even artificial) via the gastrointestinal system as long as the person lives and is not experiencing an overload of fluid (Matt. 25:44).[4]

Suggested Clarifying Statements for a Living Will

- *In the event I suffer from a cardiac or respiratory arrest and I am resuscitated and connected to life-support apparatus (that is, technology that keeps my heart pumping and lungs breathing), but I am diagnosed as being "brain dead" or in a "persistent vegetative state"—I request that the life-support apparatus be withdrawn.*

- *If the life-support apparatus is withdrawn and my heart and lungs function independently of it but I remain in a "brain dead," or "persistent vegetative state" (or I am diagnosed in the future as being in some other state, such as dementia, in which I cannot make decisions for myself), I request that I be given nutritional sustenance and hydration (whether artificial or not) via my gastrointestinal system only. I do not desire intravenous nutrition or hydration.*

- *If I continue in this unresponsive state (or other terminal state in which I cannot make decisions for myself) and I develop any future conditions that may require cardiac resuscitation, mechanical ventilation, intravenous infusions of any sort (except to control pain), surgeries (except to fix or replace a gastrointestinal tube), invasive diagnostic tests, kidney dial-*

---

[4] There are times when feeding a person via a feeding tube may cause a fluid overload in the body. If this happens, it may impair heart and lung function and do more harm than good. In such cases it may be necessary to draw back and eventually stop the feedings. It is important to remember at this point that the person's body is shutting down and is refusing the food and hydration.

ysis or antibiotics administered in any way—I refuse them all.

- *I direct all my treatment to be limited to measures that will keep me comfortable and pain free (including all prescribed medications). I expect my treating physicians to contact my healthcare surrogate (proxy) prior to any diagnostic procedures, treatments, or new medications. I also understand that as my bodily condition deteriorates, nutritional sustenance and hydration may cause complications and at such a time it may need to be gradually withdrawn and stopped.*

As mentioned earlier, in most living wills there is an area that indicates a person's desire concerning "anatomical gifts," or the donation of organs. The difficulty in this area is twofold. First, as I noted earlier, the criterion of irreversible brain damage is inadequate for Christians to accept, and this may lead to harvesting the heart and lungs of a person who is still alive! Second, in order to prevent damage to the organs and harvest them at a later time, a person is required to remain on life support until the organs are harvested, and then the person will be taken off the life support. A possibility exists that such a person could actually be alive, and by harvesting the organs, he will be put to death.

First, organs must never be harvested from a person who is diagnosed with irreversible brain damage and is not on life-support apparatus. This is murder. The second case above is not so clear-cut, however. It is my opinion that there is biblical warrant for making anatomical gifts in certain situations. Jesus does teach that "greater love has no one than this; that he lay down his life for his friends" (John 15:3). Christians are to be self-sacrificing and should *be willing to place their lives at risk* for the benefit of others. With this in mind, I believe it is okay to donate organs, provided a person is not committing suicide (Exod. 20:13) and the person is seeking to advance the kingdom of God on the earth (Matt. 6:10). Therefore, I suggest the following statement for a living will concerning the donation of organs.

- *If the life-support apparatus is withdrawn and my heart and lungs cease to function for a period of three minutes, I will consider myself dead.[5] After I am pronounced dead, I desire that my organs be preserved any way possible, and I hereby will them to any one in need of them. The person who receives my organs must be informed that my organs were given to him/her as a gift with the intent and purpose that he/she will repent and believe in Jesus Christ and will dedicate his/her life to the advancement of Jesus' kingdom on the earth.*

Selecting Healthcare Surrogates for a Living Will

Finally, when selecting people to be healthcare surrogates on a living will, make sure they are the same people listed on the durable healthcare power of attorney. Also, choose these people with great care as they may have a difficult job to do in the future. I recommend appointing one person as a primary, and a second and third as a reserve in the event the primary person is not available. It is also extremely important to sit down with healthcare surrogates, go over the living will with them, and answer any questions they may have. Healthcare surrogates have a difficult job, as they may be making life-

---

[5] Most bodily organs will not be destroyed if they do not receive blood for a period of five minutes. After five minutes, however, irreversible damage to organs will occur from lack of blood supply. If a person has not taken a breath and the heart has not had a beat in three minutes, he is dead.

and-death decisions, and they will have to live with the decisions they make on behalf of another person.

Advance Directives Integrated

A Christian should not create a durable healthcare power of attorney without a living will, and he should not write a living will without a durable healthcare power of attorney. The two may be done separately, but I highly recommend that they be completed together. No matter how well defined a living will is, questions will always be asked that require insight from a healthcare surrogate, and the surrogate will always want to know that he is representing the healthcare wishes of the person accurately. Also, I do not recommend a DNR order until a person is elderly, or has a terminal condition. Biblically, Christians should seek to prolong their lives until it is futile to do so (2 Kings 20:1-6) or until they are destroying their bodies by groping after cures (1 Cor. 3:17 NIV). It is always wise for Christians to plan ahead, however, and advance directives do just that.[6]

Due to technological advances in medicine, it is important for Christians to plan ahead. Completing advance directives will provide Christians with the assurance of biblically oriented medical care when they are incapacitated, and they will eliminate a great deal of stress on the ones they love.

---

[6] The following Web site has an integrated living will and durable healthcare power of attorney: http://www.idsos.state.id.us/GENERAL/FORMS/LivingWill_DurablePowerOfAttorney.pdf. Prior to using this form, be sure it is approved by your state.

Appendix E

Forever in His Sight:
What to Expect as a Person Approaches Death

This booklet is meant to be a guide to help you recognize the bodily changes you may observe as a person nears death. This booklet is not a checklist but a broad guide to assist in easing anxiety and to provide guidance.

It is important for you to remember throughout the dying process that although a Christian may be leaving your sight, Jesus says that he or she is forever in his sight. No matter how sick or debilitated the person may become, you can rest in this promise! The same Jesus, who said, "I am the way the truth and the life," says, "I will never leave" this Christian or "forsake" him or her. There is only one way to the Celestial City, and the Christian is on that road because of saving faith in Jesus.

Jesus gained the victory over death so that every Christian can say with the Apostle Paul,

> Where, O death, is your victory? Where, O death, is your sting? The sting of death is sin, and the power of sin is the law. But thanks be to God! He gives

us the victory through our Lord Jesus Christ. (1 Cor. 15:55-57)

Jesus already has secured the victory! Now the Christian must fight this final battle before he or she will realize the complete victory in Jesus.

Although Jesus is triumphant, this final engagement of life will still be difficult. We were not created to die. We were created to live on in eternal bliss with our bodies and souls forever. Death is the result of our sin, and at the time of death the soul is *unnaturally* ripped apart from the body. Death is always the culmination of sin and misery, for the "wages of sin is death," and that is why the dying process is characterized by pain, discomfort, misery, and suffering.

The dying process can be divided roughly into four time periods: (1) months to two weeks, (2) two weeks to one week, (3) six days to one hour, and (4) minutes. In each time period, there are identifiable signs and symptoms that are observable as a person nears death. Please remember, however, that not all signs and symptoms will be present at each state.

Months to Two Weeks before Death

During this time a person may desire to isolate himself or herself. An individual may talk less, ignore those around him or her, and lose interest in favorite activities. Weariness, fatigue, exhaustion, and a feeling of heaviness follows. Naps are more frequent, and a person may desire to stay in bed most, if not all, of the day. It is important that you continue to stay with the person, even though it seems like he or she does not acknowledge your presence. Holding hands, light massage, and touching are effective ways to communicate during this time.

You also will notice a decrease in appetite. Food provides nutrients and energy for the body. The dying person is winding down, so eating will decrease and eventually will stop. The body no longer requires food to sustain itself because it is dying. So do not be alarmed when a person stops eating.

It is important that you do not force-feed the person, as you may cause food or fluid to go into the lungs. This is the time to offer favorite foods for pleasure, not nutritional value. If the person wants to, he or she will eat it. Let the dying person decide how much and what to eat.

Two Weeks to One Week before Death

During this time period, significant changes will occur. The person will be in bed and asleep most of the time. He or she may be aroused but will return to sleep almost immediately. The person may be restless, have twitching, talk to unseen people, awake and stare off, grab at unseen objects, and attempt to remove blankets and clothing. These changes are most likely due to the body's inability to remove toxins because the organs are shutting down.

You may notice increased sweating, but the body may be cold or hot to touch. The skin may change color. If a person is feverish, he or she may appear red. The person also may appear bluish, pale, grayish, or discolored. These changes are due to a decrease in blood flow and hormonal abnormalities.

Breathing changes may occur. The person may take short, rapid breaths or stop breathing momentarily and then resume breathing again. You may notice an increase in mouth breathing and a rattling sound. The rattling is due to uncleared secretions in the lower airway and back of the throat. Breathing difficulties are caused by a number of factors, but the main problem is respiratory congestion, which is similar to drowning.

Morphine is the most effective medication to relieve suffering from respiratory congestion. The morphine is used to help the person breath more easily and more deeply. It is not used to hasten death.

Now is *not* the time to focus on the person's blood pressure and pulse. It is not necessary to take a temperature either. If a person appears rosy and is sweating, he or she probably has a fever. Giving a Tylenol suppository for a suspected fever will lessen symptoms and will provide comfort.

It will be necessary to count a person's respirations, however, because this is one of the ways the dosage of morphine is adjusted. The normal respiratory range is twelve to twenty breaths per minute, above twenty indicates respiratory discomfort.

It is also important to monitor the person for moaning, facial grimacing, and agitation, as this may indicate pain. Just because a person is sleeping or does not verbalize pain does not mean that he or she is not experiencing pain. Morphine is effective in controlling pain as well.

Six Days to One Hour before Death

As a person nears death, a sudden surge of energy may occur. He or she may be alert and appear to be doing better. The person may ask to eat a favorite meal during this time and desire company. Enjoy this grace, but please do not get your hopes up. This is a common phenomenon that indicates the end is near. This surge of energy will usually leave as quickly as it arrived, and the person will resume the one-to-two-week signs with a heightened level of intensity.

Minutes before Death

Eventually the person will slip into a coma and become totally unresponsive. Increased restlessness may be observed, and breathing may become more irregular, more shallow, and slower. Respiratory congestion may become very loud. The eyes may appear cloudy, glassy, and fixed. The hands and feet may become purplish, cold or warm, and the body sweaty, ashen, and waxy. Finally, death arrives, and the final battle is over.

The Christian will open his or her eyes and see the victor, Jesus, in all his glory sitting on his throne! Jesus will be absolutely radiant, and he will welcome the Christian to heaven. He will say, "Well done, good and faithful servant; now enter into your rest," and with a tender hand he will wipe away every tear of suffering, pain, and misery. The physical body of the Christian will be left behind to decompose. But one day, Jesus will return and miraculously resurrect the decayed body, make it a glorified body, and reunite it to his or her glorified soul. Then the Christian will live on in the Celestial City with recreated body and soul forever in his sight.

This booklet is meant to be a guide to help with the recognition of physical and mental changes that may occur as a person approaches death. These changes are not definitive, and this is not meant to be a comprehensive guide. It is intended to help you understand what is happening to the person who is dying and to alleviate stress.

It is also important that you do not become preoccupied in looking for these changes. These are the final days of the dying person's life, so cherish your final days and hours together, and do not cease to meditate on the sure hope of eternal life with Christ.

Summary of Signs and Symptoms
Months to Two Weeks
1. Isolation and withdrawal
2. Poor appetite
3. Increased sleep
4. Less communication

Two Weeks to One Week
1. Confusion
2. Restlessness

3. Talking to unseen people (hallucinations and delusions)
4. Pulling off blankets and clothing
5. Physical signs and symptoms
   A. Color changes to the skin
   B. Increased sweating
   C. Irregular breathing
   D. Congestion and raspy breathing
   E. Sleeping but responding to touch
   F. Complaints of the body feeling heavy and fatigued
   G. Insignificant food and fluid intake
   H. Body temperature may be either hot or cold

Six Days to One Hour
1. Sudden surge of energy
2. Intensification of one-to-two-week signs and symptoms
   A. Glassy eyes, cloudy, tearing, fixated, and half open eyes
   B. Irregular breathing patterns with long pauses between breaths
   C. Increased restlessness or no movement at all
   D. Purplish feet and hands

Minutes
1. Gasping for air like a fish out of water
2. Totally unable to be aroused
3. Cold, clammy, pale, gray, ashen, or bluish body

Appendix F

Going into God's Presence

If you are reading this booklet, you are either curious about its content, or you have been diagnosed with a life-limiting illness. If your answer is the latter, you may be experiencing a myriad of thoughts, feelings, and emotions. You may also have physical pain and discomfort, and everything about this experience may be overwhelming. Perhaps you fear the days ahead, and you have many questions. The goal of this pamphlet is to provide answers for some of your questions, in the hope that you may find comfort and guidance in the midst of this final trial of life.

A Myriad of Thoughts, Feelings, and Emotions

Usually after a person receives a terminal diagnosis, disbelief, shock, and denial occur. Your mind may be racing, and you may feel confused. Perhaps the whole matter seems surreal. These thoughts and feelings will be short-lived, however, and eventually, they will be joined by anger, anxiety, fear, and depression.

You may be prescribed medications to help you cope with these emotions and feelings, but medications will not be enough. You will also require counseling. It is important for you to know that counseling is always based upon the underlying convictions of your counselor, no matter how hard the counselor may try to follow your beliefs about life, death, and the hereafter. A simple statement like, "Don't worry; everything will be okay," is a statement of belief. In our culture people view life and death in different ways, and the way they understand and treat feelings and emotions accompanying death will be just as unique. This pamphlet will provide you with counsel about life, death, and the hereafter that is rooted in orthodox and traditional Christianity. The Bible teaches that Jesus is God, and at a certain time in human history, he became a man. Jesus lived in our world as *the only* perfect man, and at the age of thirty-three, he was crucified for our sins. After Jesus died, he was buried, and three days later he rose from the dead, conquering sin, death, and the devil. In his resurrected body, he ascended into heaven and sat down at God's right hand.

The Bible also teaches that people will either receive or reject these facts about Jesus. If they are received, when a person dies, his or her soul will go to be with Jesus in heavenly bliss. If they are rejected, when a person dies, his or her soul will be separated from Jesus and will enter hell. Then, one day in the future, Jesus will come again to judge everyone and make all things new. At his second coming, a bodily resurrection will occur, and everyone who ever existed will stand before Jesus with a reunited body and soul. Those who received him will be acquitted on the basis of his righteousness and reenter heaven with a resurrected body and soul. Those who rejected him will be condemned on the basis of their unrighteousness and will reenter hell to endure infinite suffering in their bodies and souls.

These are the fundamental doctrines of the Christian religion, and if you believe them, then you have a firm foundation for comfort and hope in the midst of this trial. You know what will happen after you die, no matter how you may feel or whatever emotions you may experience, and no matter how sick you may become, Jesus is always with you. Jesus says to you even now,

> Come to me . . . you who are weary and burdened, and I will give you rest. Take my yoke upon you and learn from me, for I am gentle and humble in heart, and you will find rest . . . My yoke is easy and my burden is light. (Matt. 11:28-30)

Certain types of medications may help to settle your mind, and as a result, it may be easier for you to find rest in Jesus. Use the recommended medications as an aid that will help you to read, meditate on, and pray over the gracious promises found in the Bible. You may still struggle with shock, bewilderment, denial, confusion, anger, anxiety, fear, and depression, but know also that if you are yoked to Jesus, these thoughts, feelings, and emotions are yoked to him as well, and one day the suffering will all be gone. The Bible is tried and true counsel for your heavy-laden soul, so go to Jesus in faith and rest in him.

Physical Pain and Discomfort

You have probably experienced pain and other symptoms due to your disease already. It is important for you to know that uncontrolled pain and discomfort can affect your thoughts, feelings, and emotions as well. There are several medications and ways to treat pain and discomfort, but it will be necessary for you to report what you are experiencing to your nurse.

The type of pain you have, whether it is dull, deep, achy, burning, shooting, tingling, or numbing, will help the nurse know what kind of medication to use. The location and severity of your pain is important to report. Usually, the nurse will ask you to rate your pain on a scale from one to ten, with ten being the worst possible pain you have ever had.

This information helps to determine the class and dosage of medication to use. Once a pain-management plan is in place, it is important to report any episodes of continued pain, what you were doing when you experienced the pain, and any side effects from the medications you are taking. It is equally important to take the medication on a consistent schedule, as the schedule helps to keep a steady level of the drug in your bloodstream in order to treat the pain adequately.

You may be afraid of some of the medications used, especially morphine. These medications are used to alleviate pain and suffering, and that is all. They are not used to hasten death. Like all medications they must be monitored carefully and adjusted appropriately to control your pain. Initially, after taking certain pain medications, you may experience sedation and a feeling of euphoria, but these side effects will usually wear off in a few days. Also, don't be afraid of becoming addicted to the medication. You require the medication to treat your pain at present and to assist you in devotion to God, to your family, and to your friends.

Finally, it is important that you do not skip a scheduled dose of medication or stop taking it because you are pain free. If you are pain free, it is probably because the present medication and dosage is effective. If you stop abruptly, you may experience withdrawal symptoms, and your pain may return with a vengeance. If this happens you may require different medications to control the withdrawal and higher doses of narcotics to control the pain.

Some of the other symptoms that may cause you discomfort and can be treated are: restlessness, agitation, confusion, hallucinations, difficulty sleeping, constipation, diarrhea, decreased appetite, difficulty swallowing, upset stomach, nausea, vomiting, cough, hiccups, a painful mouth, upper respiratory congestion, shortness of breath, fevers, and seizures. It is important for you to report any of these or other symptoms to your nurse. The goal is to increase your quality of life, which means treating pain, suffering, and discomfort so that you may be able to rest easier in Jesus.

Getting Things in Order

Quite often it is at times like these that issues that may have been hidden or pushed away for many years may come back and bother you. Sometimes people feel guilty because of something they have done to God or another person in the past. Perhaps, you have done all that you could to submerge this guilt, to numb it, to forget about it, but there it is again gnawing at you. If you are experiencing guilt, God may be telling you something; he may be telling you that something is not right with your relationship to him or others.

The only way to deal with guilt is to confess it to God. The Bible says if you confess your sins, which are what causes the guilt, he is "faithful and just" to forgive them (1 John 1:9). So confess your sins to God, and he will forgive you. Then, if it is possible and if you are able to do so, seek reconciliation with those you may have sinned against. Perhaps, you have sinned against a spouse, a child, a friend, or a neighbor; seek their forgiveness as well. It is important to remember that if you seek reconciliation with God and others with a sincere heart, then you are forgiven, even if you still feel guilty. In such instances, cling in faith to the gracious promise of God that "he is faithful and just to forgive," and not to your feelings.

On a completely different note, it is important for you to choose a healthcare proxy. A healthcare proxy is a specific person you identify to speak on your behalf if you are unable to do so. I recommend you pick one person as a primary and a second and a third as backup. It is extremely important for you to communicate to your healthcare proxies your wishes concerning your medical care and to be sure that the proxies are people who can carry out what you want. The healthcare proxies have a difficult job, as they may be making life-

and-death decisions on your behalf. If it is your desire to let your terminal disease run its course, to be as comfortable as possible, without any aggressive medical treatment, then communicate these wishes to your healthcare proxies.

Another important part of preparation is getting your estate in order and planning your funeral. One of the blessings of knowing how long you have to live is that you have time to prepare to die. Getting things in order will help those close to you immensely and will relieve a great deal of future stress for those you care about. If you have not prepared a will and settled your finances, now is the time to do so. It is also time to prepare your funeral. How will your service be organized? Who do you want to perform the service? What Scripture verses will be read? By taking these steps, you will care for, witness to, and encourage your family and friends in a profound way.

As Death Nears

In this section I will briefly present some of the things that may occur as death nears. This is not meant to scare you but to help you with the unknown. At one to three months before death, you may desire to withdraw from people and prefer to lie or sit quietly alone. You may experience a decrease in appetite, and any food you do eat may make you feel extremely tired. You may want to sleep more, and you may have less interest in your favorite activities. At one to two weeks before death, your body may begin to feel heavy, and you will be fatigued after movement. You may become disoriented, confused, agitated, have bizarre dreams, and hallucinations. Your heart may beat faster. You may experience breathlessness. You may feel changes in your body temperature. Within days to hours of death, you may have a sudden surge of energy, but this will be followed by a decline to coma and eventual death.

As Eternal Life Nears

If you rested in Jesus, after you die you will open your eyes in eternity and see him in all his glory! You will enter heaven, and before you Jesus will be seated on his glorious throne. He will be absolutely radiant, and he will welcome you to heaven. You will also see a rainbow over his throne, and gathered around it will be twenty-four elders dressed in brilliant white robes with golden crowns on their heads. You will see and hear them worshiping Jesus constantly, saying: "You are worthy, our Lord and God, to receive glory and honor and power, for you created all things, and by your will they were created and have their being" (Rev. 4:11).

In front of Jesus' throne, you will see seven blazing lamps and a sea of glass as clear as crystal. Above and around the throne, you will see four angelic creatures. The first has the face of a lion, the second like an ox, the third like a man, and the fourth like a flying eagle. Each of these angelic beings has glistening scales and six wings, and they fly around Jesus. Constantly, they offer praise to Jesus saying, "Holy, holy, holy is the Lord God Almighty, who was, and is, and is to come" (Rev. 4:8).

If this is not enough, Jesus will descend from his glorious throne and come to you personally. As he approaches, he will say to you, "Well done, good and faithful servant, now enter into your rest" (cf. Matt. 25:21, 23). Then he will draw near, and with a tender hand, he will touch your eye and wipe away every tear of suffering, pain, and misery. Then he will say to you, "There will be no more death or mourning or crying or pain" (cf. Rev. 21:4), for you have entered into the fullness of life and joy.

Those Left Behind

The most important thing you can do for those who will be left behind is to engage in open and honest communication with them, especially the children who are close to you.

It may be difficult, and it may cause many tears, but talk about your terminal diagnosis and impending death. Don't hide that you are dying; don't feel like you have to be strong for others. Talk about how you feel and talk to the children at a level that they can understand. Keeping open lines of honest, heartfelt communication will pay off with huge dividends when you are gone, particularly for the children.

I said, at the beginning of this booklet, my goal was to provide you with hope, comfort, and guidance in the midst of this final trial of your life here on earth. It is my prayer that this objective has been reached. I leave you with these words of encouragement from the Apostle Peter:

> Praise be to the God and Father of our Lord Jesus Christ! In his great mercy he has given us new birth into a living hope through the resurrection of Jesus Christ from the dead, and into an inheritance that can never perish, spoil or fade – kept in heaven for you, who through faith are shielded by God's power until the coming of the salvation that is ready to be revealed in the last time. In this you greatly rejoice, though now for a little while you may have had to suffer grief in all kinds of trials. (1 Pet. 1:3-6)

Appendix G

Life's Final Trial: Devotions for Faith, Hope, and Assurance

Life's Trials

And we know that in all things God works for the good of those who love him, who have been called according to his purpose.

(Romans 8:28)

If you have been newly diagnosed with a terminal disease, you may be saying to yourself,
"This is the last passage I want to read right now. How can all of this work together for good? Look, I am suffering. I will soon be separated from the people I love. I am dying! Why would you select a passage like this to provide comfort?"

You are faced with a difficult trial, yes, but a trial that God promises to use for your good and for the good of everyone who loves him, "who have been called according to his purpose."

Christians believe that nothing is left to random chance. We believe and affirm God's providence. Christians believe in God's most holy, wise, and powerful control over the entire universe, including your specific trial right now. Notice the text says, "In all things God works," not in some things, but in everything. God is at work in all things and working them out "for the good of those who love him" and "who have been called according to his purpose." The "good"—that is, the best possible goal for God's children—is always to glorify him. It is for this reason that God has brought this final trial into your life at this time.

Ultimately the text is saying that God is doing this for your good! How, you ask? God is causing you to consider your hope. Is your hope in him or in someone or something else? God is making you less dependent upon the world and more dependent upon him. God is using this trial to bring you into his presence. It is to this final trial to which you have been called at present, not to death as an end in itself, but to eternity.

Prayer

O great Triune God of all power, rule, control, and governance, we are humbled by your incomprehensible purposes. Father, I pray for your afflicted servant during this difficult time. Help your servant to rest in you, and help your servant to know that all of this is happening for good—for your good. I pray this in Jesus' name, amen.

Praise

When peace, like a river, attendeth my way, When sorrows like sea billows roll;
Whatever my lot, Thou has taught me to say, It is well, it is well, with my soul.
Refrain:
It is well, with my soul, It is well, with my soul, It is well, it is well, with my soul.

Though Satan should buffet, though trials should come, Let this blest assurance control,
That Christ has regarded my helpless estate, And hath shed His own blood for my soul.
Refrain

My sin, oh, the bliss of this glorious thought! My sin, not in part but the whole, Is nailed to the cross, and I bear it no more, Praise the Lord, praise the Lord, O my soul!
Refrain

For me, be it Christ, be it Christ hence to live: If Jordan above me shall roll, No pang shall be mine, for in death as in life Thou wilt whisper Thy peace to my soul.
Refrain

But, Lord, 'tis for Thee, for Thy coming we wait, The sky, not the grave, is our goal;
Oh trump of the angel! Oh voice of the Lord! Blessèd hope, blessèd rest of my soul!
Refrain

And Lord, haste the day when my faith shall be sight, The clouds be rolled back as a scroll; The trump shall resound, and the Lord shall descend, Even so, it is well with my soul.
Refrain

—Horatio Spafford, "It Is Well with My Soul"

*****

Life's Guide

Your word is a lamp to my feet and a light for my path.

(Psalm 119:105)

When people follow medicine as a guide, they are doomed to hopelessness. Medical science can only treat symptoms and stave off the inevitable for a period of time. One day the unavoidable will arrive for everyone—death will come. Medical science is not a guide that can be trusted. Its light is dim, and it leads ultimately to disappointment.

On the other hand, the psalmist says that God's Word illuminates the way ahead clearly. God's Word, of course, is found in no other place but the Bible. "All Scripture is given by inspiration of God," says the Apostle Paul (2 Tim. 3:16). The Bible is God's Word, because God communicated it to us. The Apostle Peter says that holy men spoke as they were moved by the Holy Spirit to do so, and it is these words that are written down in the Bible (2 Pet. 1:21). God's Word can guide us because it is infallible—it is a perfect guide for faith, life, and practice. It shows us what life is really about and how we are to live. The Bible is a lamp to our feet and a light to our path. It leads us moment by moment and provides clear illumination for the pathway ahead. In God's Word the path is not obscure, dark, and hopeless; it is clear, illumined, and hopeful.

Trust in the LORD with all your heart and lean not on your own understanding; in all your ways acknowledge him, and he will make your paths straight. (Prov. 3:5-6)

Prayer

O blessed and almighty God, God of guidance and light: Father, I pray for your servant. I pray that you would lead and guide your servant into all truth, comfort, and assurance of the hope found only in Holy Scripture. Illuminate each step of the way and light up the road ahead. Grant, Father, bright meditations on the radiant and glorious New Jerusalem that awaits your servant at the end of this difficult road. I pray in Jesus' name, amen.

Praise

Before Thee let my cry come near, O LORD; true to Thy word, teach me. Before Thee let my pleading come; True to Thy promise, rescue me.

Since Thou Thy statutes teachest me, O let my lips Thy praise confess. Yea, of Thy word my tongue would sing, For Thy commands are righteousness.

Be ready with Thy hand to help, Because Thy precepts are my choice. I've longed for Thy salvation, LORD, And in Thy holy law rejoice.

O let Thine ordinances help; My soul shall live and praise Thee yet. A straying sheep, Thy servant, seek, For Thy commands I ne'er forget.

—Psalm 119:169-176 (The Book of Psalms for Singing)

*****

Life's Faith

For it is by grace you have been saved, through faith—and this not from yourselves, it is the gift of God.

(Ephesians 2:8)

In his letter, James, Jesus' brother, says that "every good and perfect gift comes from above," that is, from God (James 1:17). Jesus Christ is God's greatest gift to mankind. The familiar verse, John 3:16, says, "God so loved the world that he sent his only begotten Son into the world." It was the Father's desire to send Jesus, his Son, into the world as a gift to mankind.

There is no fact more clearly attested in human history than the Son of God coming into the world. Two premier Jewish and Roman historians of Jesus' day, Josephus and Suetonius, mention him in their writings. It is the Bible, however, that testifies to the life of Christ. Luke, the physician, evangelist, and respected historian from Syria in Jesus' day, wrote his gospel to provide an "orderly" and exacting "account" of Jesus' life on earth. Luke's historical record describes what Jesus came to do, so that we may understand, believe, and trust the saving work he did on our behalf.

According to Luke, Jesus was born in Bethlehem under the reigns of Claudius Caesar and Herod the Great. Jesus was supernaturally implanted by the Holy Spirit in the womb of a Jewish virgin named Mary. He was born of her and was without sin. Jesus lived for thirty-three years in the region of Palestine, and during those years he kept every detail of God's law perfectly. He had to fulfill all the requirements of the Old Testament law system, and he had to be presented to God as a perfect offering without sin.

During his brief life, he confronted the hypocritical religious establishment, gathered followers, preached a message of repentance, and performed many miracles. He ushered in the kingdom of God on earth. The religious officials hated Jesus for all these things, so they plotted to kill him. Jesus was betrayed by one of his close associates, was arraigned by a kangaroo court, and was sentenced to death by crucifixion under the Roman governor Pontius Pilate. Although innocent, Jesus willingly accepted this punishment, and he was executed outside the city walls of Jerusalem in AD 33. He received the punishment that we deserve for our lawlessness, guilt, and sins, and he died on our behalf. The grave could not hold Jesus, however; on the third day, he rose from the dead!

It is the gracious work of the Father and the Son that saves us. The Father did not have to send his Son into the world, nor did the Son have to come and die in our stead. This grace saves us by faith. Faith is a gift of God as well. It is the instrument that links us to what Jesus did on our behalf many years ago. Faith has three components: knowledge, assent, and trust. You have to know who Jesus was, what he did, and what you are being saved from in order to be saved. You have to give assent to these facts and believe them to be true. Then, you have to trust these facts, and that means basing your entire life upon them. This is the grace that truly saves, because it originates with God and not with us.

Prayer

O Glorious God, author of salvation, praise to your name. Thank you for your Son Jesus Christ, your gift to the world. Lord Jesus, thank you for obeying your Father, and being willing to suffer and die an awful death on our behalf. Thank you Holy Spirit for the application of the Father's grace, salvation, and faith—all free gifts given to us at the cost of your beloved Son. Amen.

Praise

O sacred Head, now wounded, with grief and shame weighed down, now scornfully surrounded with thorns, thine only crown; O sacred Head, what glory, what bliss till now was thine! Yet, though despised and gory, I joy to call thee mine.

What thou, my Lord, hast suffered was all for sinners' gain: mine, mine was the transgression, but thine the deadly pain. Lo, here I fall, my Savior! 'Tis I deserve thy place; look on me with thy favor, vouchsafe to me thy grace.

What language shall I borrow to thank thee, dearest Friend, for this, thy dying sorrow, thy pity without end? O make me thine forever; and should I fainting be, Lord, let me never, never outlive my love to thee.
— *"O Sacred Head, Now Wounded"*

*****

Life's Hope

To them God has chosen to make known among the Gentiles the glorious riches of this mystery, which is Christ in you, the hope of glory.
(Colossians 1:27)

Hope is help in the midst of life's final trial. You have great hope, for God has said that he will never leave you or forsake you (Heb. 13:5). He has given you the gift of his Son, and he has "chosen" you to be his child. He also has "chosen" you for a purpose, and that is to "make known" the glorious mystery of "Christ in you, the hope of glory." These are stupendous and hopeful words!

The author of the book of Hebrews says that "faith is being sure of what we hope for and certain of what we do not see" (Heb. 11:1). Your present hope is that Christ is in you, and this is revealed by your faith in him. If you possess this present hope, then you have power to endure under this present trial. In fact, this present hope will be an anchor for your soul.

Now if we are children, then we are heirs—heirs of God and co-heirs with Christ, if indeed we share in his sufferings in order that we may also share in his glory. I consider that our present sufferings are not worth comparing with the glory that will be revealed in us. (Rom. 8:17-18)

Christian hope is both a present reality and a future promise. It is not a vague, "I wish" or "I think," but it is a firm assurance that what God promises is true. Christian hope is a present power, a sure anchor, and a certainty of greater things to come. Beloved, you possess "the knowledge of the truth that leads to godliness—a faith and knowledge resting on the hope of eternal life, which God, who does not lie, promised before the beginning of time" (Titus 1:1-2). So fix your "eyes not on what is seen, but on what is unseen, for what is seen is temporary, but what is unseen is eternal" (2 Cor. 4:18). Right now you see but a poor reflection as in a mirror, but one day you will come face to face with Jesus. Presently, you know the mystery only in part, by faith, but one day you will know it fully, even as you are fully embraced by Jesus, and this is your hope of glory!

Prayer

Merciful Father, I pray for faith and hope to fill the soul of your servant. Grant, Holy Spirit, great assurance of everlasting life in Christ. Reveal more clearly the present reality of Christ in your servant, and open your servant's spiritual eyes to the "hope of glory" to come. I pray this in Jesus' matchless name, amen.

Praise

My hope is built on nothing less than Jesus' blood and righteousness; I dare not trust the sweetest frame, but wholly lean on Jesus' name.
Refrain:
On Christ, the solid rock, I stand; all other ground is sinking sand, all other ground is sinking sand.

When darkness veils his lovely face, I rest on his unchanging grace; in every high and stormy gale, my anchor holds within the veil.
Refrain

His oath, his covenant, his blood support me in the whelming flood; when all around my soul gives way, he then is all my hope and stay.
Refrain

When he shall come with trumpet sound, O may I then in him be found; dressed in his righteousness alone, faultless to stand before his throne.
—Edward Mote, "The Solid Rock"

*****

Life's Love

Now these three remain: faith, hope and love. But the greatest of these is love.

(1 Corinthians 13:13)

The Bible says that Jesus is love, for "God is love." In 1 Corinthians 13, if you exchange the word *love* with the name of *Jesus,* you will possess a portrait of his loving character. Jesus is patient, and he is kind. Jesus does not envy, he does not boast, and he is not proud. Jesus is not rude, nor is he self-seeking. He is not easily angered, and he keeps no record of wrongs. Jesus does not delight in evil but rejoices with the truth. He always protects, always trusts, always hopes, and always perseveres. Jesus never fails. Christian, it is this same love that has started to shine forth in your own life, that grows brighter and brighter each and every day. Love is the greatest power that you possess, for it is the very love of Jesus that has been given to you from the Spirit of Christ.

Jesus' love outlasts everything. When faith and hope are weak, love will still burn within your heart. One day faith will become sight. "We shall see him as he is" (1 John 3:2), and faith will fade away. On that same day, hope will become a reality, and this too will pass away. But love will endure forever and ever throughout all eternity. Our love for Jesus and his love for us begins now, and it will never end, even after we die! It will only become deeper and more intimate. So, when you start to doubt and despair in the midst of this final trail of life, remember the love of Jesus, this same love he has given to you.

Who shall separate us from the love of Christ? Shall trouble or hardship or persecution or famine or nakedness or danger or sword? . . . No, in all these things we are more than

conquerors through him who loved us. For I am convinced that neither death nor life, neither angels nor demons, neither the present nor the future, nor any powers, neither height nor depth, nor anything else in all creation, will be able to separate us from the love of God that is in Christ Jesus our Lord.
(Rom. 8:35-39)

Prayer

O loving Jesus, you are love, and you possess perfect love, and you give love. I pray for your servant. I pray that your servant may know the power of your love during this difficult trial. I pray that your servant's love may abound more and more in desire for you. I pray that when things may seem dark and hopeless, that your love would prevail in the heart of your servant. Amen.

Praise

Jesus, lover of my soul, let me to thy bosom fly, while the nearer waters roll, while the tempest still is high: hide me, O my Savior hide, till the storm of life is past; safe into the haven guide, O receive my soul at last!

Other refuge have I none, hangs my helpless soul on thee; leave, ah! leave me not alone, still support and comfort me! All my trust on thee is stayed, all my help from thee I bring; cover my defenseless head with the shadow of thy wing.

Thou, O Christ, art all I want; more than all in thee I find; raise the fallen, cheer the faint, heal the sick, and lead the blind. Just and holy is thy name; I am all

*unrighteousness; false and full of sin I am, thou art
full of truth and grace.*

*Plenteous grace with thee is found, grace to cover
all my sin; let the healing streams abound; make and
keep me pure within: thou of life the fountain art,
freely let me take of thee; spring thou up within my
heart, rise to all eternity.*
　　　　　—Charles Wesley, "Jesus, Lover of My Soul"

*****

Life's Promise

**For no matter how many promises God has made,
they are "Yes" in Christ. And so through him the
"Amen" is spoken by us to the glory of God.**
　　　　　　　　　　　　　(2 Corinthians 1:20)

Jesus is the foundation, bedrock, and bulwark for all of
God's promises. "And so through him the 'Amen,'" that is,
the "let it be so," or truly, "is spoken by us to the glory," or
praise, "of God." Consider this promise of Jesus in the midst
of this final trial of your life:
Do not let your hearts be troubled. Trust in God; trust also in
me. In my Father's house are many rooms; if it were not so,
I would have told you. I am going there to prepare a place
for you. And if I go and prepare a place for you, I will come
back and take you to be with me that you also may be where
I am. You know the way to the place where I am going. (John
14:1-4)

God in his grace through Jesus Christ has granted you faith,
hope, and love in this life so that you may embrace the future

promises that are mentioned in this passage. The road is coming to an end, and your destination point is just around the corner. It is hard to wrap your mind around what Jesus is saying, but remember the one who is saying it is the basis for all of God's promises. He says to you even right now, "Trust me."

Christian, after this final trial, your soul will go to God's house in heaven, and at a future date, your body will rise, as a renewed glorified body, and be reunited to your soul. Then, for all eternity you will have eternal rest and peace, both in your body and in your soul. The veritable and trustworthy Jesus, the one in whom all of God's promises are "yes" and "amen," promises it. What better guarantee can you have than this?

And I heard a loud voice from the throne saying, "Now the dwelling of God is with men, and he will live with them. They will be his people, and God himself will be with them and be their God. He will wipe every tear from their eyes. There will be no more death or mourning or crying or pain, for the old order of things has passed away." (Rev. 21:3-4)

I declare to you, brothers, that flesh and blood cannot inherit the kingdom of God, nor does the perishable inherit the imperishable. Listen, I tell you a mystery: We will not all sleep, but we will all be changed—in a flash, in the twinkling of an eye, at the last trumpet. For the trumpet will sound, the dead will be raised imperishable, and we will be changed. For the perishable must clothe itself with the imperishable, and the mortal with immortality. When the perishable has been clothed with the imperishable, and the mortal with immortality, then the saying that is written will come true: "Death has been swallowed up in victory." Where, O death, is your victory? Where, O death, is your sting? The sting of death is sin, and the power of sin is the law. But thanks be to

God! He gives us the victory through our Lord Jesus Christ.
(1 Cor. 15:50-57)

Prayer

O the riches of the glory of God! Your ways are past
finding out. All of your promises are yes and amen
in Jesus. Lord Jesus, thank you for your faithfulness,
hope, and love on our behalf. Holy Spirit, thank you
for communicating the faith, hope, and love of Christ
to us so that we may know, believe, trust, embrace,
strive after, and be assured of God's future promises
to come. Grant your servant the ability to meditate
deeply on the promises of heaven and the bodily
resurrection. Yea, though outwardly we are wasting
away, yet inwardly we are being renewed day by day.
Amen.

Praise

*Glorious things of thee are spoken, Zion, city of our
God; he whose word cannot be broken formed thee
for his own abode: on the Rock of Ages founded,
what can shake thy sure repose? With salvation's
walls surrounded, thou may'st smile at all thy foes.*

*See, the streams of living waters, springing from
eternal love, well supply thy sons and daughters, and
all fear of want remove: who can faint, while such a
river ever flows their thirst t'assurage? Grace which,
like the Lord, the giver, never fails from age to age.*

*Round each habitation hov'ring, see the cloud and
fire appear for a glory and a cov'ring, showing that
the Lord is near: thus deriving from their banner
light by night and shade by day, safe they feed upon
the manna which he gives them when they pray.*

Savior, if of Zion's city I, through grace, a member am, let the world deride or pity, I will glory in thy name: fading is the worldling's pleasure, all his boasted pomp and show; solid joys and lasting treasure none but Zion's children know.
—John Newton, *"Glorious Things of Thee Are Spoken"*

*****

Life's Fulfillment

I tell you the truth, he who believes has everlasting life.

(John 6:47)

Jesus is life. Speaking to the grieving Martha, whose brother had just died, Jesus said, "I am the resurrection and the life. He who believes in me will live, even though he dies; and whoever lives and believes in me will never die" (John 11:25-26).

Jesus is the author of life. Everything that has life has it because Jesus gives it. Christianity is not just one way to life among many; it is the only way to true life, because Jesus is the creator and re-creator of all life. Jesus says, exclusively, "I am the way and the truth and the life" (John 14:6). Dear Christian, if you remember anything at all, remember this: you have this life. No matter how fearful and difficult this trial may become, your death opens the door to eternal life.

Death cannot destroy the life that Christ has given to you. The life that Jesus gave to you is everlasting; it will never end. You have been delivered from sin and death to righteousness and life. It is a life that begins here and now and is lived according to the Bible, in faith, hope, and love. It is a life that will spring up into eternal and everlasting life that will never end. Death is not death for you; it is the final trial of this life that swings open the door to eternal life.

Then all of this will make sense to you. You will see how God orchestrated his perfect plan for your life on earth. When an artist creates a Persian carpet, he will hang it from a scaffold and work at the carpet from one side. The artist will have his apprentices on the other side of the carpet handing him different colored threads—yellow, red, brown, and black. The artist will stitch the thread in a pattern on the front side of the carpet, but on the back side the apprentices will see only several multicolored threads in a tangled mess. When the carpet is finished, however, the artist will instruct his apprentices to come over to the front side and see the finished product. On the other side of the rug, the pattern is beautiful; all of the yellow, red, brown, and black threads are arranged perfectly. So it will be when you enter eternal life; you will see God's perfect plan and not a thread of suffering, misery, or pain will be out of place.

> For we know in part and we prophesy in part, but when perfection comes, the imperfect disappears . . . Now we see but a poor reflection as in a mirror; then we shall see face to face. Now I know in part; then I shall know fully, even as I am fully known. (1 Cor. 13:9-12)

Prayer

Most gracious God, glory and praise to your name. Lord Jesus, thank you for everlasting life. I pray for your servant that you will be pleased to grant greater assurance of eternal life, in the midst of this final trial of life on earth. Amen.

Praise

I love the LORD, because He hears my pleading. He's heeded me; through life I'll call on Him. The cords of death and Sheol's terrors bound me; In deep distress I grief and trouble found. Then on the LORD's name in prayer I called: "You I implore, O LORD, deliver my soul!"

The LORD your God is merciful and righteous; Gracious, the LORD the simple ones preserves. When I was low, to me He gave salvation. Turn back again, my soul, unto your rest, Because the LORD has dealt well with you, Because my helpless soul You rescued from death.

You saved my eyes from tears my feet from stumbling. Before the LORD I'll walk in lands of life. I have believed and said, "I am afflicted." I in despair confessed "All men are false!" What shall I render now to the LORD For all his benefits upon me bestowed?

Salvation's cup I'll lift up in the LORD's name, vows to the LORD before his people pay. Observed by Him and precious in the LORD's sight Appears the death of all His saints each one. O LORD, I am Your servant, Your slave. I am Your handmaid's son, for You set me free.

To You I'll bring my off'ring of thanksgiving; With sacrifice I'll call upon the LORD. I'll pay the vows I made unto Jehovah before His people all, O may it be! With in His courts the house of the LORD, In midst of you, Jerusalem! Praise the LORD!
          —Psalm 116 (The Book of Psalms for Singing)

End Notes

Introduction

[1] See appendix A for a *Pastor's Medical Handbook,* which is a summary of the pages to follow. The handbook is a helpful tool to keep on hand during the medical rotations or in a medical counseling session.

1. Western Medicine is NOT Neutral!

[1] Paul Vitz, *Psychology as Relgion: The Cult of Self-Worship* (Grand Rapids: Eerdmans, 2002), 117.

[2] Ibid., 118.

[3] Ibid., 113-14.

[4] It is important to distinguish between what I call microbiological death and biological death. In the garden, Adam, Eve, and the animals ate plants, so this required the death of the plant for digestive purposes on the microbiological level. So death in one sense always existed prior to the fall. The Bible teaches that biological death—that is, the death of a living species with blood in it—did not occur until after the fall (Gen. 2:17; Lev. 17:11; Rom. 6:23).

[5] There are basically two biblical positions that try to explain the origin and transmission of the soul to subsequent generations. The first position is called traducianism. This view suggests that just as the material parts of the body came from the parents to the child, so does the immaterial soul (cf. Gen. 46:26; Heb. 7:10). The major problem with this view is maintaining the sinless incarnation of Christ. The second, and most common, position is called creationism. According to this view, each individual human soul is created directly by God and implanted in each individual person at the time of conception (cf. Heb. 12:9; Eccles. 12:7; Ps. 139:13-14). The major difficulty with this view is how a good God could create a sinful soul. In support of this view, it must be remem-

bered that sin occurs in subsequent generations because of affiliation with Adam's first sin (Rom. 5:12), not because God created a sinful soul, or body, for that matter.

6 John Cooper, *Body, Soul & Life Everlasting: Biblical Anthropology and the Monism-Dualism Debate* (Grand Rapids: Eerdmans, 1989), 42.

7 Louis Berkhof, *Systematic Theology* (Grand Rapids: Eerdmans, 1996), 203.

8 Charles Hodge, *Systematic Theology*, vol. 2, *Anthropology* (Peabody, MA: Hendrikson, 1999), 97.

9 Berkhof, *Systematic Theology*, 205.

10 Meredith Kline, *Images of the Spirit* (Eugene: Wipf and Stock, 1980), 23.

11 Ibid, 24.

12 John 1:1-4, 9, 14.

13 Berkhof, *Systematic Theology*, 205.

14 J. P. Moreland and Scott B. Rae, *Body & Soul: Human Nature & the Crisis in Ethics* (Downers Grove, IL: InterVarsity, 2000), 202.

15 Ibid, 205.

16 Cooper, *Body, Soul, & Life Everlasting*, 228.

17 Thomas Boston, *Human Nature in its Fourfold State* (Grand Rapids: Associated Publishers, Inc., n. d.), 8.

18 Ibid, 9.

19 Bruce Waltke, *Genesis A Commentary* (Grand Rapids: Zondervan, 2001), 86.

20 Ibid.

21 Josh. 11:11ff.; 1 Kings 15:29; 17:17; Job 27:3; Ps. 104:29; Isa. 2:22; cf. Gen. 2:7; 6:17; 7:15, 22; Ezek. 37:5ff.; Acts 17:25.

22 The full report can be found at: https://idea.iupui.edu/dspace/handle/1805/707.

3. Body, Soul, Medications, and Biblical Counseling

1 Robert E. Enck, *The Medical Care of Terminally Ill Patients* (Baltimore: John Hopkins University Press, 2002), 34.

2 Gen. 6:5; Deut. 15:9; 1 Chron. 29:18; Esther. 6:6; Job 17:11; Ps. 64:6; Jer. 23:20; Dan. 2:30; Matt. 15:19; Mark 7:21; Luke 9:47; Acts 8:22; Heb. 4:12.

3 I am speaking here of the normal means of grace. In cases of those who are infants, mentally retarded, deaf, and blind, God works as he pleases. It is important to note, however, that he always saves people the same way, no matter what their condition may be. There must be conviction of sin, knowledge of the saving work of Christ, repentance, and the

embracing of his saving work. It is certainly possible for a sovereign God to work all of this immediately inside the souls of such people if he so chooses, but this is not his normal means of working. Normally, God will use the sensory organs, particularly the ears and eyes, to communicate his saving truth to people.

4 Ronald Wallace, *Calvin's Doctrine of the Word and Sacrament* (Eugene: Wipf and Stock, 1997), 2.

5 Quoted in Morton Smith, *Systematic Theology* (Greenville, SC: Greenville Seminary Press, 1994), 2:610.

6 John Calvin, *Commentary on Isaiah* (Grand Rapids: Baker, 1999), 172.

7 John Calvin, *Institutes of the Christian Religion,* ed. John T. McNeill (Louisville: John Knox Press, 1960), 4:14:17.

8 Ibid., 4:14:4.

9 Wallace, *Calvin's Doctrine of the Word and Sacrament,* 135.

10 Quoted in Ibid., 137.

11 Neil Williams, *Gospel Transformation* (Jenkintown, PA: World Harvest Missions, 2006), 196.

12 Ibid.

13 John 14:12; Rom. 1:5; Gal. 5:6; Eph. 3:16-17; 1 Thess. 1:3; 2 Thess. 1:11; 1 Tim. 1:3-4; Heb. 4:2; 11:6; 1 John 5:4.

14 Williams, *Gospel Transformation,* 324.

15 Ibid., 345.

16 2 Cor. 1:22; 5:5.

17 Williams, *Gospel Transformation,* 240.

18 Sinclair Ferguson, *The Holy Spirit: Contours of Christian Theology* (Downers Grove, IL: InterVarsity Press, 1996), 249.

19 John 11:4; 12:16, 23, 28; 13:31-32.

20 Ferguson, *The Holy Spirit,* 252.

21 The twofold effect of the gospel is in view here (2 Cor. 2:15-16).

22 It is very important for the pastor to discern between what are called symptoms (subjective findings) and signs (objective findings). Technically, in order for a disease to be diagnosed, factual evidence (blood pressure, lab tests, MRI, etc.) must exist. The medical community has a tendency to label subjective complaints (symptoms) as a disease without any objective findings (signs), and this is wrong. Alcoholism and a plethora of psychological conditions are examples of so-called diseases that are diagnosed from subjective data.

23 Robert Smith, *The Christian Counselor's Medical Desk Reference* (Stanley: Timeless Texts, 2000), 49–51. It is not necessary to know

the dosages, but it is important to understand why the medication was prescribed and any side effects noted.

[24] This is not to suggest that the spit, clay, and water did anything (Jesus could have healed with a spoken word if he wanted to), but it does show that Jesus is not adverse to using the elements in the creation.

[25] I understand that a pastor is not a medical doctor, and it will be difficult to assess these matters. It is at this point, however, that a pastor will benefit from exposure to, and integration into, the member's healthcare team. The pastor cannot prescribe and should not withdraw medications, but he can refer the member he counsels, along with his *objective* assessment (i.e., insomnia, hands are tremulous, cannot keep a conversation, alert but disorientated to person, place, and time, reports, "I will die if I stop taking my antianxiety medication," wringing of hands, lying about . . . , itching, etc.), to various healthcare professionals who can.

[26] It is extremely important that the pastor recognize his boundaries at this point. He should never make the decision to pursue or not to pursue medical intervention. The pastor should act as a guide who provides factual information in light of medical findings and provides counsel that is biblical. Ultimately, the person or his family must make the final decision to pursue or to forgo medical treatment. This does not mean, however, that a pastor does not give his opinion in light of medical findings but only that he should not make the decisions for the parties involved.

[27] See appendix B for an annotated summary of Charles Spurgeon's excellent sermon "Songs in the Night." This sermon has some excellent advice on how to counsel those who are ill, diseased, or facing death. ay

4. Making Decisions Regarding Medical Care

[1] See also the parallel accounts in Matt. 9:2-8 and Luke 5:18-26.

[2] All illness and disease ultimately is caused by evil, or sin, but there is not always a one-to-one correspondence between personal sin and the immediate affliction.

[3] http://www.aa.org/bigbookonline/en_BigBook_chapt5.pdf

[4] In my experience, I have come across many Christians who think that they have an excuse to stop ministering when they become ill, contract a disease, or even face death. This kind of thinking is radically unbiblical (cf. Job 2:10; the supreme example to the contrary is Christ on the cross: Luke 23:24, 39–43; John 19:25–27; Matt. 26:53–54). Although it may be a struggle to cope under these afflictions and still minister, the excuses not to minister are based on sentimentality and a low view

of God's providence. As long as a Christian is in a state of consciousness, he should seek to minister to others, even if that means a deathbed ministry of prayer. For a powerful testimony to God's sustaining grace in one man's deathbed experience that still ministers to us today, see the *Memoirs of Thomas Halyburton*, ed. Joel R. Beeke (Grand Rapids: Reformation Heritage Books, 1996), 226–94. See also appendix C for an annotated summary of Thomas Halyburton's deathbed experience.

[5] William Bridge, *The Works of William Bridge* (Beaver Falls, PA: Soli Deo Gloria Publications, 1989), 2:191.

[6] Richard Baxter, *The Saints Everlasting Rest*, abridged version by Benjamin Fawcett (Ann Arbor: Cushing – Malloy, 1978), 245. I took the liberty to update the language in the quotations.

[7] Ibid.

[8] Ibid,, 246.

[9] Ibid, 264.

[10] Robert Smith, *The Christian Counselor's Medical Desk Reference* (Stanley: Timeless Texts, 2000), 31.

[11] Ibid., 41.

[12] See Paul's example in 2 Cor. 11:9; 12:13-14, 16.

[13] See this Web site for your state's advance directives: http://www.caringinfo.org/stateaddownload. See also appendix D for a copy of an available booklet called *The Christian and Advance Directives*.

[14] Another helpful document that is now recognized in forty states is the *5 Wishes* advance directive: http://www.agingwithdignity.org/5wishes.pdf. Although the document is humanistic, it may serve as a good outline for Christians as they seek to develop there own well-defined advance directives.

5. Pastoral Care and Counseling at End of Life

[1] Elisabeth Kübler-Ross, *Death: The Final Stage of Growth* (New York: Simon & Schuster, 1975), 2.

[2] Elisabeth Kübler-Ross, *On Death and Dying* (New York: Macmillan, 1969) 39, 140.

[3] Ibid., 39.

[4] Ibid., 50.

[5] Ibid., 83.

[6] Ibid., 87-88.

[7] Ibid., 112-13.

[8] In 1995 Dr. Kübler-Ross encountered her own mortality when she suffered a series of strokes, and in August of 2004 death summoned her. During her final days, Kübler-Ross's sister was irritated by the way she

desired to live on in this present world. Her sister said in an interview, "She wrote so much about death and dying, glorified it even. And now her time has come and she says, 'I still have to do this and that.'" If this is truly the case then, it appears that Kübler-Ross did not accept death at all. In fact, it seems that she lived an entire life characterized by denial, and in the end, when her hope of death arrived, she was riveted to this present life.

[9] Kübler-Ross, *On Death and Dying*, 112.

[10] Enck, *The Medical Care of Terminally Ill Patients* (Baltimore: John Hopkins University Press, 2002), 171.

[11] It is important to mention that when a person is in an unconscious state, he or she will still experience pain and discomfort. This is usually evident through wincing, irritability, picking, rapid breathing, raspy breathing, and moaning. Also, the nurse is skilled at assessing pain and discomfort. The nurse should establish this baseline with the patient right away and also should explain that as the disease progresses and death nears, more medication may be required to alleviate pain and discomfort. The main thing the pastor needs to do is to make sure a biblical balance is maintained and the dying person is not overly influenced by the nurse, who will be inevitably biased in his or her approach.

[12] The pastor should never assume that he knows the level of suffering or pain a person is experiencing. Pain, discomfort, and suffering are subjective and are always what the person says they are.

[13] The individual may report having guilt, remorse, visions, bizarre dreams, and visitations from people he was acquainted with who have already died. These may be important areas where repentance and forgiveness are needed, especially if guilt and remorse is the cause. On the other hand, these experiences may be pleasant, such as experiences of the heavenly reality to come or a reunion with long-dead saints. It is important for the pastor to explore these things with the member and to recommend the use of medication wisely. Do not write off dreams, visions, or other experiences too quickly, because these experiences are doorways into the subconscious world of the dying individual (I do not mean to sound Freudian or Jungian!), and they will help the pastor to counsel effectively.

[14] Several booklets are available thorugh Christian Community Care to assist the pastor, patient, and family with end of life issues. See appendices: E, F and G.

[15] This is not a rigid schedule, because each situation is unique. Visits should be based on the family's needs.

[16] Moving on with life does not mean doing away with memories. In fact, tapping into memories can be a good way to get people to grieve and move on with their lives.

Breinigsville, PA USA
12 April 2010
235946BV00005B/1/P